# SIMPLE PRINCIPLES™
## TO EXCEL AT SCHOOL

Alex A. Lluch
**Author of Over 3 Million Books Sold!**

Dr. Helen Eckmann
Doctor of Education and Leadership Science

WS Publishing Group
San Diego, California

SIMPLE PRINCIPLES™
TO EXCEL AT SCHOOL

By Alex A. Lluch and Dr. Helen Eckmann

Published by WS Publishing Group
San Diego, California 92119
Copyright © 2008 by WS Publishing Group

Designed by WS Publishing Group:
David Defenbaugh

For Inquiries:
Log on to www.WSPublishingGroup.com
E-mail info@WSPublishingGroup.com

ISBN13: 978-1-934386-22-4

Printed in China

# TABLE OF CONTENTS

# INTRODUCTION

In past decades, excelling at school was encouraged only for upper-class men who wanted to be professionals. It was not critical for women, who were encouraged to take up domestic work, or middle- and lower-class men, who were supposed to enter trade fields, to indulge in education. However, in the 21st century, excelling at school is not only a matter of survival, it is crucial to achieving success in a competitive world. *Simple Principles™ to Excel at School* will give you the secrets to mastering your schoolwork, getting into a great college, and thus creating the foundation for a life of success.

Many people believe that their achievements at school are limited by their natural talents and abilities, even their genetics. Nothing could be further from the truth! Every single student can excel at school provided they are willing to learn the principles contained in this book. This book will teach you habits and attitudes that will improve your ability to study, read, write, score high on tests, become organized, adopt responsibility, cope with anxiety, develop healthy habits for learning, set sound educational goals, and get into college. Adopting these habits will absolutely result in your improved performance in school. You may be surprised where this newfound success might take you. Have you always thought you were not smart enough to be a professor? Think again — all it takes is applying the principles in this book. Is it your dream to become a doctor? You have the power to get there, and will reach your goal by following the wisdom of these principles.

**What is this book about?**

In short, this is a book about becoming a great student. In more depth, this is a book about developing a deep appreciation and respect for learning and the habits that can achieve this mindset. It is about learning new skills, including taking notes, participating in class, becoming an analytical reader, writing well-researched papers, and studying for tests. This book also offers information on how healthy habits, such as eating well, getting exercise, sleeping enough, and having a healthy social life, can maximize your success as a student. Finally, this book is about maximizing your brainpower, self-esteem, mental faculties, and environment to result in a more fulfilling, more productive, and more successful academic career. Use this book as a tool to help you become the student you have always wanted to be.

It is important to remember that your performance in school will likely have ups and downs. It is impossible to pass every test, ace every paper, and excel in every class. Part of being a successful student is weathering the setbacks and having patience with your learning abilities. Avoid putting too much pressure on yourself — but be sure to put enough pressure that you are motivated to do your best, try your hardest, and learn something new every day.

This book addresses ways in which you can become a stronger student. Before you start, however, it is important to recognize the things about yourself that cannot be changed, and factor them into your expectations and work plan. For example, you cannot control the fact that a foreign language may not come naturally to you. However, you do have control over how much time you put into your French homework, whether you get a

French tutor, or whether you stay after school to meet with your teacher about work that is giving you trouble. This book will help you figure out how to go the extra mile in subjects that have thus far eluded you.

This book emphasizes the role that positive thinking and a healthy lifestyle play in your overall academic success. Several principles included in this book guide you away from destructive, unhealthy, or unproductive behaviors that interfere with your ability to concentrate and learn. There are also principles to help you learn how to change your mind about your natural talents and ability to succeed academically. Finally, there are principles that offer advice on social, physical, and dietary habits to adopt if you want to have an easier time excelling in school.

**Who should read this book?**

This book is for students who want to:

- Learn ways to become organized
- Create a work space that facilitates learning
- Cut down study time by maximizing study habits

- Become a critical reader
- Improve note-taking skills
- Go up at least 1 whole grade in every class
- Write effective 5-paragraph essays
- Learn researching skills
- Take the stress out of tests
- Identify their academic strengths and capitalize on them
- Identify their academic weaknesses and support them
- Know what healthy dietary, physical, and social habits support learning
- Reduce their anxiety over school-related matters
- Learn how to deal with peer pressure
- Articulate short- and long-term educational goals
- Know where to go to help when they get stuck
- Improve their chances of getting into college
- Involve their parents in their education

Lastly, this book is for people who want to be able to flip to a page that applies to their situation and find an inspirational tip that will quickly put them on the road to becoming a better student.

## Why should you read this book?

You should read this book because excelling in school is one of the single greatest things you can do to improve your life in the immediate present and in decades to come. Even if you consider yourself to be a good student already, there is something in here for you — a study tip you haven't thought of or a fact about the college admissions process you can benefit from. You should also read this book because it combines much wisdom into easy-to-read simple principles. In general, if you want to get the most out of your education and to invest in a bright future for yourself, you should read this book.

To know whether this book is right for you, here are some questions to ask yourself:

- Do you have trouble concentrating?
- Do you have trouble understanding your teachers' lectures?
- Is it difficult for you to remember and apply what you read?
- Could your writing skills stand to be improved?
- Is there a particular subject that you shy away from?

- Are you uncomfortable participating in class?
- Do you often feel bored in class?
- Do you hate going to school?
- Are you burdened by peer pressure?
- Are you constantly late or disorganized?
- Do you have a hard time settling into your work?
- Do you have a work space that facilitates learning?
- Does your diet and exercise regimen undermine your ability to learn?
- Are you unsure of what you'd like to do in the future?
- Are you worried you won't be accepted to the college of your choice?

If you answered "yes" to any of these questions, then this book is for you. These are just a few of the many topics covered in this book. The principles contained in this book are researched and supported with inspirational quotes and statistical information from credible sources. Its size makes it easy to keep with you for easy reference or for a quick pick-me-up in the middle of the day. You should read this book whenever you are ready to make changes and improve your overall educational performance.

# Why is it so difficult to be a great student?

Being a successful student is exceedingly challenging in today's schools. School overcrowding and underfunding has resulted in classrooms that lack proper equipment and teacher-student interaction. In fact, in some states, the student-teacher ratio is so disproportionate that classes see as many as 40 students enrolled. Competing for a teacher's attention with 39 other students is difficult and students are not likely to receive individual attention. Therefore, students must learn strong academic skills on their own, since they cannot rely solely on their teachers.

Another reason succeeding in school has become a challenge is student apathy. The results of an extensive and ground-breaking 2007 study that surveyed more than 81,000 students found that the overwhelming majority of students are bored in school because they dislike the material and have inadequate interaction with their teacher and other students. When students get bored with school, they become less likely to participate in the extracurricular activities that are critical for developing healthy social and physical habits to support their academic success. A snapshot of students in Minnesota helps us get a glimpse of the extent of student apathy: Among male students in the Minnesota study, 19.1 percent engaged in neither sports nor other activities, 23.4 percent in other activities only, 15.1 percent in sports only, and just 42.4 percent of all male students participated in both an athletic sport and an extracurricular activity. That's more than half the male student body that refrains from participating in just one sport and one other extracurricular activity! Female students were found to be only slightly more engaged with school and school-related extracurricular activities; among female students, 12.6 percent were involved in neither, 31.6 percent in other activities only, 7.3 percent in sports only, and 48.6 percent in both.

Against this backdrop, school testing has become more rigorous and important. The passage of the No Child Left Behind Act has made standardized testing a frequent and important part of the curriculum. Finally, with more and more people going to college, getting an advanced degree has become a more competitive process that many young students are ill-prepared for.

Clearly, a mix of overcrowding and underfunding in schools, student apathy, and more stringent academic requirements places an extraordinary burden on our children, causing them to struggle in school.

## Why is it important to excel at school?

These challenges are difficult, but students must remember the single most important reason to excel at school: because it pays. According to a 2004 report by the U.S. Department of Commerce, those with no high school education earn an average of $26,879 per year. Those with a high school diploma can expect to earn about $37,031 per year. Completing a portion of college will garner a person about $44,312 per year, while a bachelor's degree puts a person's average annual salary at $67,495. Put another way, a 2007 College Board study found that people with a bachelor's degree earn over 60 percent more than those with only a high school diploma. Over a lifetime, the gap in earning potential between a high school diploma and a B.A. is more than $800,000. There is even more money to be made if you advance academically beyond the college level — according to the National At-Risk Education

Network, a master's degree is worth an additional $13,000 per year, and a professional degree is worth a whopping $24,000 more per year.

With tens of thousands of dollars at stake, and with industries become increasingly competitive due to foreign outsourcing and automation, you can't afford not to excel at school.

However, the importance of securing a financially comfortable future is just one part of why it is important to excel at school. The other reason is because learning is a lifelong pursuit that has the ability to enrich not only your wallet, but your heart, mind, and soul. When you fall in love with learning, you develop a relationship with people from the past; with organisms so small you can't see them; with countries around the world; with planets galaxies away! In other words, learning exposes you to life, the world, imagination, the past, the present, and even the future. It allows you to develop your imagination, creativity, and your role in the human story.

The best thing about becoming a better student is that once you discover your love of learning, you will never let it go.

Once you get a taste of what it feels like to be a critical thinker, an expert in a field, and a generator of unique, creative, sharp ideas, you never want to go back to your old ways. Learning enriches the whole of a person's life. As the great writer Oliver Wendell Holmes once put it, "Man's mind, once stretched by a new idea, never regains its original dimensions." *Simple Principles™ to Excel at School* will help instill this love of learning in you and couple it with an understanding of how to do your best in school. After practicing the principles contained in this book, most students will realize that their ultimate goal is to become a lifelong learner. You will know that learning does not stop when one graduates from school or finishes a course. Learning does not ever have to stop — and how wonderful that is the case!

**What do you need to know to become a better student?**

There is a lot you need to know in order to become an excellent student, and this book simplifies the enormous amount of information for you.

This book offers the following tools to help you excel at school:

- Advice on how to create a work space that facilitates learning
- Tips for maximizing what you learn in class
- Ways to develop effective study skills
- Exercises that promote organization and responsibility
- How to read, write, and communicate effectively
- How to prepare for exams
- How to minimize the stress you feel before tests
- Healthy habits for learning
- Tools for controlling school-related anxiety
- Places to seek support when you get stuck
- How to identify your academic strengths and weaknesses
- How to deal with peer pressure
- Ways to make friends
- How you can come to love going to school
- How you should approach the college application process

This book also will teach you that:

- Believing that you can become a great student is important.
- Learning can be a fun, interesting, and satisfying endeavor.
- Controlling your stress directly affects your ability to perform well in school.
- Eating well and getting exercise directly affect your ability to perform well in school.
- Respecting your peers, parents, and teachers is important for self-respect.
- You can dramatically improve your grades by changing your study habits.
- If you follow the principles found in this book, there is no subject you cannot learn!

Use the simple principles in this book as you would a toolbox. Refer to them often as you need them. Eventually the tips in this book will become second nature and you will find yourself advancing academically — and even enjoying the process of learning.

# Maximizing the Benefits of This Book

Always keep this book handy. Keep it in your backpack or school bag. Put in the glove compartment of your car. Stick in the top drawer of your desk in your room. Lay it on your nightstand before bed. This book is written to be read over and over again. The principles will take time to affect change, so the idea is to read and practice them often. Remember that your pursuit to become a better student is a long-term goal that will take time and effort. However, you will put yourself on the road to academic success the second you begin reading this book.

# CREATING A HOME LEARNING ENVIRONMENT

We tend to overlook the impact our environment has on us. But our surroundings infiltrate our attitude and inspire us, for better or worse. Creating an environment that facilitates learning is key ingredient for becoming a successful student.

An example of how important the right learning environment is comes from the Department of Education in Alberta, Canada. Officials there conducted a two-year study involving different kinds of light used in classrooms. Researchers found that the type of light used in a classroom has an enormous effect on students' scholastic achievement, growth and development, attendance, and even their physical health. Students performed poorly under fluorescent and halogen lighting, exhibiting hyperactivity and an inability to concentrate. But under full spectrum light with trace ultraviolet rays, students learned faster, scored higher on tests, had 33 percent fewer absences due to illness, and 66 percent fewer health problems such as cavities.

In another study on students in Florida, lead researcher Dr. John Ott found that proper lighting can even improve the performance of students with learning disabilities. Concluded Ott, "Several extremely hyperactive children with confirmed learning disabilities calmed down completely and rapidly overcame their learning and reading problems while in the full spectrum lighted environment. The overall average academic achievement level showed significant improvement."

Proper lighting is just one important component of a home learning environment. The following simple principles explore many others. We recognize that not every household will be able to implement every idea listed here. For those principles that you cannot apply in the home, look to the public or school library to supplement. Just try to adopt as many of the following principles as you can to create an environment that facilitates learning.

# Principle #1

## Work at a large and uncluttered desk.

One of the most important elements of your home learning environment is your desk. Think of your desk as your studying headquarters. It is as critical to your ability to do homework as a cockpit is critical to a pilot who needs to fly. Feng Shui design techniques recommend that desks be placed in the northwest sector of a room. Be sure to keep your desk neatly organized and free of clutter. Says Tabitha Miller, a Feng Shui consultant who specializes in student work spaces, "Clutter is an enemy of Feng Shui, because it represents too much yin energy, which brings feelings of confusion, tiredness, and procrastination."

# PRINCIPLE #2

## Keep necessary equipment nearby.

It will be impossible to settle into your homework if every 10 minutes you go off searching for a ruler, eraser, or new sheet of graph paper. Be sure to organize your work space so all equipment needed for work is within arm's reach. Items such as pens, pencils, dictionary, thesaurus, textbooks, assignment books, paper, calculator, ruler, crayons, index cards, scissors, folders, highlighters, tape, paperclips, wall calendar, and notebooks should be stored in an organized fashion in your desk or around your work space.

# Principle #3

## Keep your study space
## noise free.

Carving out a quiet, private place to study and do homework can be difficult in most homes. According to researchers with TV Turnoff Week, the average American household has the television on more than 50 hours per week! Furthermore, if you are like 80 percent of Americans who live in urban or suburban places, you are constantly bombarded with the noise of car horns, garbage trucks, or landscaping equipment. An environment in which there is constant noise is not a place that will facilitate learning. If you cannot make a noise-free study space at home, head to the library where you are guaranteed a quiet environment.

# Principle #4

## Let the right sounds in.

While a quiet, noise-free study space is optimal, it doesn't necessarily have to be sound-free. Sounds are waves that travel through the air. When these waves hit your body, they affect your mood, concentration, focus, and outlook. Listening to certain sounds while studying can actually improve your concentration and memory. Wind chimes, soft bells, or the sounds of nature, such as a babbling brook, are all conducive to studying. Music without lyrics, such as jazz, ambient, or classical music, has the same effect. Multiple studies have shown that listening to classical music during tests improves students' scores. As the philosopher Plato once said, "Music is a more potent instrument than any other for education."

# PRINCIPLE #5

## Create an ergonomic work space.

Have you ever felt pain in your wrist, shoulder, or elbow after using the computer or reading for a long time? Most likely, these aches can be attributed to a work space that is not ergonomic. Ergonomics refers to the design of a work area that helps maximize the efficiency and quality of work. Ergonomic work spaces are designed to minimize discomfort and fatigue. The most critical component of your ergonomic work space is your chair. Make sure your chair has arm rests, is level with your desk, and allows you to sit straight up, rather than lounging. If you work at a computer, use a wrist rest. Designing an ergonomic work space will allow you to focus on studying rather than how uncomfortable you are.

# Principle #6

## Allow fresh air and sunshine to enter your study space.

If possible, create your study space in a room that receives fresh air and sunlight. Studies show that students who work in classrooms that receive natural light score 20 percent higher on math tests and 26 percent higher on reading tests than in classrooms that get no daylight. Author Zane Madison writes, "A good breath of fresh air can revitalize, energize, and stimulate the mind that has been dulled, as well as the body that is fatigued." If fresh air and sunshine are available to you, use them to improve your study sessions.

# Principle #7

## Green your study space.

Adding indoor plants to your study space has several benefits for your ability to learn. Plants absorb carbon dioxide and turn it into oxygen, which stimulates your brain and helps you think clearly. Plants also metabolize a host of toxins found in most homes, helping to purify the oxygen you breathe. An ongoing study by NASA has found that many kinds of houseplants help filter chemicals such as benzene, trichloroethylene, and formaldehyde out of the air. Green is also a soothing color that promotes calm and relaxation, which will help you feel less stressed as you work. Plants are an inexpensive and easy way to add vitality to your work space.

# Principle #8

## Color your environment for learning.

Decorate your work space with colors that are conducive to mental stimulation and concentration. Color therapy, or phototherapy, is a growing scientific field that has proven that certain colors trigger hormonal responses in humans. For example, the color red stimulates brain wave activity, increases heart rate, and boosts energy levels. Yellow is also a good choice because it has been shown to energize people, relieve depression, promote clarity, and improve memory. Choose these shades when decorating your study space. Avoid shades of indigo, which help the mind enter a meditative state, or blue, which triggers coolness and rest.

# Principle #9

## Always study in a well-lit environment.

———————— ✳ ————————

In addition to studying in a space with natural lighting, use lamps to illuminate your work space. When students work in an improperly lit space, their eyes get tired very easily. The muscles of the eyes tend to stiffen in dim spaces. Flexibility of the eye muscles is important for sharp thinking and reading. The light used should be bright but glare-free — squinting will give you a headache. Feng Shui design techniques recommend avoiding fluorescent lighting because it interferes with learning. In fact, a study of Florida students revealed that first-graders who work in classrooms with fluorescent lighting are more hyper than students who work under lamps that duplicate natural sunlight.

# Principle #10

## Get online.

An increasing number of high schools and even middle schools are taking their course content to the Internet. Teachers frequently use the Internet to post homework assignments and other materials available for student download. Other types of online work, such as message-board posting or Web-based project research, are increasingly part of the 21st-century curriculum. Make sure your home computer has a fast Internet connection and the most up-to-date Web browsers and software (new versions are usually available free online). If you don't have a home computer, go to your school or public library. They will likely have several stations you can use.

# Principle #11

## Strive for a distraction-free work space.

※

Writer Robert Bloch once astutely noted, "Any occurrence requiring undivided attention will be accompanied by a compelling distraction." Indeed, a work space is useless if it is smack in the middle of distractions. Obviously you will have difficulty absorbing the causes of the Vietnam War if the TV is playing in the background and you are instant messaging with your best friend. To spend quality time working, turn off the TV. Sign out of email. Turn off your cell phone. Avoid surfing the Web. If your study space has a door, hang a sign on it to let housemates know you are working and should not be disturbed.

# Maximizing What You Learn in Class

If going to class was all it took to excel at school, then all students who simply showed up would get the same grade. But just being present in class does not guarantee you will get anything of value from it. In order to become a successful student, you must learn how to maximize your time in class.

The results of an extensive and ground-breaking 2007 study offer some indication of how students spend their time in class. The study, which surveyed students from 110 high schools, found that the overwhelming majority of students are bored in class because they dislike the material and have inadequate interaction with their teacher and other students. A whopping 66 percent of students said they are bored in at least one of their classes, while 17 percent of students said they are bored in every class.

What most students don't realize, however, is that they hold the key to making class more interesting. They can do this with one simple act: participation! Without a doubt, class participation is one of the best weapons against in-class boredom. The best students know it not only earns them grade points, but makes class time more interesting, fulfilling, and satisfying. When you participate, you can impact the direction of the class discussion. You can get involved in the ideas being discussed. You can voice your own opinions, and hear what your teacher and fellow students think of them.

With this in mind, never let a class go by without making a contribution. Come to class prepared so you can actively engage those around you in the material. Don't be afraid to voice your opinion about the material — start a heated debate over whether genetic engineering is moral, for instance. It will make for a much more interesting class than simply sitting back and watching the clock tick. Most of all, your fellow students, and especially your teacher, will appreciate your zeal for learning.

Class participation is just one way you can maximize your time in class. The following simple principles explore ideas for making class time interesting, useful, and most of all, educational.

# Principle #12

## Complete all assignments — before class starts.

The most important thing you can do to maximize what you learn in class is to come prepared. Being prepared means completing all assignments and readings before class. This will help you understand that day's lesson and allow you to participate by making helpful comments and asking insightful questions. Coming to class prepared will also help the notes you take make more sense. If you can't finish all the reading by the time class starts, skim parts you weren't able to get through by reading the first sentence of every paragraph, the table of contents, and the book's introduction.

# Principle #13

## Get to class a few minutes early.

Getting to class on time is not only polite, but helps you improve your grades. Teachers take off points for lateness and will reduce your grade if you habitually show up late. But being in your seat before the bell rings has many benefits. If there are notes on the board, you can copy them before class begins so you don't have to listen and copy at the same time. Getting to class early also allows you to look over notes from the previous class session so you can be prepared for the upcoming lecture. Coming to class early also allows you the time to discuss any thoughts or questions you might have with fellow students.

# Principle #14

## Have the right equipment.

American storyteller Louis L'Amour once said, "Opportunity knocks all the time, but you have to be ready for it. If the chance comes, you must have the equipment to take advantage of it." The same is true for class. If you go to class lacking the proper equipment, you will be unable to take advantage of the ideas and skills being taught. Therefore, always show up with the proper equipment. At the very least, this means a notebook, pens, pencils, calculator, and any handouts or books related to the day's lesson. If the class session requires special equipment — such as materials for an experiment — get these in advance.

# PRINCIPLE #15

## Come to class with at least 3 questions.

The 18th-century philosopher Voltaire once advised people to "judge others by their questions rather than by their answers." Indeed, teachers tend to judge the most successful students by the quality of questions they ask. For this reason, always come to class with at least 3 good questions. These could be thought-provoking questions about a piece of text you read, or you could inquire about the teacher's opinion. You could pose a question to students in the group, or ask the teacher to clarify something you didn't understand. The act of questioning forces you to engage in the material. If you make it a habit to come to class with a few prepared questions, you will quickly see your grades soar.

# Principle #16

## Become an active listener.

Amazingly, students get about 75 percent of their knowledge from actively listening to others. Actively listening involves looking at the person who is talking and carefully considering their comments without thinking of what you will say next. It means listening to a comment in its entirety, not just part of it. Active listeners refrain from being restless or fidgety while others are talking. According to education experts James and Constance Messina, the brain can process more than 5 times as many words per minute as can be spoken, which means zoning out is simply wasting an opportunity to learn and reduce future study time outside of class. Stay active by asking questions, taking notes, and retaining a speaker's key points.

# Principle #17

## Avoid recording lectures.

Too often students record a lecture rather than taking notes. However, handwritten notes have been shown to embed lessons more firmly in a student's mind than listening to recorded material. Furthermore, handwritten notes can be referred to quickly, rather than searching through a recording for a specific point. Writing instructors at Dartmouth College have said, "A student who takes the easy way out — recording the lecture on tape as he or she sits back doing nothing — will box him or herself into inflexibility." If you record a lecture, take notes at the same time. Use the recording only to help fill in sections of the lecture that went too quickly for you.

# PRINCIPLE #18

## Turn off all handheld and portable devices.

It should seem obvious that class is not the place to be text messaging or fiddling with your MP3 player. Yet a frightening number of students use handheld portable devices in class, to their own educational detriment. According to a 2005 study by MIT, 41 percent of students admitted to using their cell phone to check messages while in class. However, most students know this is inappropriate; 96 percent of students said they thought it was wrong or unacceptable to use a cell phone in class. To get the most out of class, turn off all handheld portable devices and turn your attention where it should be: your studies.

# Principle #19

## Always take notes.

─────────────── ✳ ───────────────

A shocking number of students fail to take notes during class. "In every one of my classes," says veteran teacher Kim Turner of San Francisco, "there is at least 1 student who sits there with his notebook open but nothing written down." Students who do not take notes are significantly less likely to do well in school. The act of writing down information helps cement it in your mind. In fact, you are much more likely to remember something you have written down than something you have simply heard. Taking notes also shows your teacher you are interested in the lecture. He or she will remember this effort when grades are handed out.

# PRINCIPLE #20

## Have separate notebooks for each class.

— ✳ —

It should go without saying that you should keep notes for each class together and separate from other sets of class notes. Yet too many students fail to keep individual notebooks for each class. Serious students keep class notes organized. They never scribble notes on random pieces of paper — these get lost, and are usually difficult to integrate into the other notes taken for the class. Successful students also date their notes, and number the pages of their notebooks consecutively, like a real book. This helps them find information quickly and keep information in order.

# Principle #21

## Avoid creating a transcript of the lecture.

It is less important to take notes on every word the teacher says than it is to write down the important ones. Teachers usually give clues about what is worth writing down. These include material written on the board; words, ideas, or phrases the teacher repeats or speaks with emphasis; and information included in previews given at the beginning of a lecture or summaries at the end of a lecture. Quotes, rules, definitions, laws, or formulas should, however, be written down exactly as your teacher says them. But for most ideas, avoid creating a transcript of the lecture and concentrate instead on absorbing the most important ideas.

# Principle #22

## Develop a note-taking shorthand.

People can speak faster than they can write, and because of this, many students find it difficult to keep up with taking notes while their teacher talks. That's why it is important to develop a note-taking shorthand. Use abbreviations when necessary. Some common abbreviations are: "e.g." for example; "w/ or w/o" for with or without; "re:" for regarding; "b/c" for because; "b/t" for between; and many others. In addition to abbreviating words, abbreviate your thoughts. Never use a sentence where you can use a phrase, and never use a phrase where you can use a word. Develop a uniform system of punctuation and abbreviation that will make sense to you. For additional suggestions, visit www.nldline.com/notetaking_tips.htm.

# Principle #23

## Let the speaker's visual clues guide you.

When taking notes, pay attention to the body language and vocal inflections your teacher demonstrates as he or she presents the lecture. Speakers often give visual clues that will help you figure out which material is most important to write down. Look for gestures, facial expressions, particular pauses, and how dramatically or quietly your teacher makes his or her points. Each of these will give you clues as to how important the material is and help reinforce it in your mind. To ensure you are able to pick up on a speaker's visual clues, be sure to get a seat with an unobstructed view that is as close to the front of the class as possible.

# Principle #24

## Pay attention to the visual aids.

It is rare that a teacher simply stands in front of the class talking. Lectures are often accompanied by visual aids such as pictures, slides, diagrams, charts, or transparencies. More modern classrooms may have technology that allow teachers to project the image of a Website onto a large screen or wall. Burying your head in your notebook will cause you to miss valuable information. Remember, teachers use visual aids because they are a part of the lecture, not a side note. Avoid getting so wrapped up in your note-taking that you forget to look up to experience other components of the lecture.

# Principle #25

## Don't be afraid to ask for clarification.

Some teachers lecture at breakneck speed, almost as if they forget students are listening to them. If your teacher is covering material too fast, do not hesitate to interrupt him or her. Ask for clarification of a particular topic, term, or idea that you didn't understand. Request that he or she repeat a statement. It can be difficult to draw attention to yourself by asking the teacher to slow down, but chances are you are not the only one missing out on the material. Your classmates will be grateful that you put the brakes on the lecture.

# Principle #26

## Revisit your notes as soon as possible.

An excellent way to reinforce class material is to recopy, rework, or otherwise revisit your notes once you get home from class. Revisiting your notes helps you better remember the day's material. Also, out of the class environment, you can take more time to absorb the material. Were there certain terms used in the lecture that you did not understand? Now is a good time to look them up. Were you unfamiliar with a person or event that was mentioned? Research the unfamiliar topic, and include it in the margins or other white spaces of your notes. The goal of revisiting your notes while the material is still fresh in your mind is to create the best set of notes possible for later, when you don't remember the material as well.

# Developing Study Skills & Doing Homework

A frustrating aspect of studying and doing homework is that after 2 hours of working, you are not guaranteed to have accomplished anything significant. Unfortunately, studying is not the sort of activity you can punch the clock on. The good news is that by learning study skills you can trade quantity of hours put in for quality of work accomplished. Depending on how sharp your study skills are, you may accomplish as much in 1 hour as someone with poorer skills might accomplish in 1 day.

Interestingly, trends in education over the past 20 years have put much emphasis on test scores, but less emphasis on homework. The No Child Left Behind Act is one piece of educational policy that backs the idea that student test scores are the best indicators of learning. But many prominent academicians remind both students and parents that time spent doing daily homework should not be overlooked, as it is this work that can most contribute to a student's overall academic success. According to Brian Gill of RAND Corporation and Steven Schlossman of Carnegie Mellon University, "To succeed, academic excellence movements ultimately require students to invest effort in their studies; time spent on homework is a ground-level indicator of this effort."

However, research shows that American students are not hitting the books as often as needed — and when they do study, they are not getting much bang for their buck. According to 2003 data analyzed by the Brown Center on Education Policy, the great majority of students at all grade levels spend less than 1 hour studying and doing homework on a typical day. Studying isn't just putting in time with your books and notes — it is what you do with them that matters. If you dislike doing homework, think of an old Philippine proverb that goes, "The bitterness of studying is preferable to the bitterness of ignorance." Time spent studying and doing homework is critical for becoming a better student. The following simple principles will teach you study skills and homework techniques that will help you get the most out of the time you invest in your education.

# PRINCIPLE #27

## Study a little bit every day.

———————————— ✳ ————————————

When a test looms in your future, you will need to use a different set of skills and techniques (for more on getting ready for exams, see the chapter Getting Ready for an Exam). You can minimize your work and stress levels before tests by studying a little bit each day. Take 15 minutes out of every homework session to review the day's notes. Recopy sections that are messy and add information to sections that are incomplete. Numerous studies have shown that the brain retains information learned slowly over time better than when it is bombarded by information at the last minute. Learn for the long term by studying a little bit every day.

# PRINCIPLE #28

## Make use of mnemonics.

— ❊ —

Memorization techniques, known as mnemonics, are word formations that link something you need to learn with something you already know. For example, you might use a mnemonic to memorize a list or order of operations. Countless students have used the mnemonic HOMES to remember the names of the Great Lakes: Huron, Ontario, Michigan, Erie, and Superior. Similarly, music students have long relied on the acrostic "Every Good Boy Deserves Fudge" to remember the notes in the musical scale, E, G, B, D, and F. Come up with your own mnemonics to memorize material, and get creative! Some students have had success making word-association raps or singing to the tune of a familiar song.

# Principle #29

## Let others know you are not to be disturbed.

Ralph Waldo Emerson once wrote, "Concentration is the secret of strengths in politics, in war, in trade, in short in all management of human affairs." Emerson intimately understood the importance of being able to concentrate and became one of America's most beloved essayists. He was known to be extremely focused and not to allow anyone to interrupt his work. Indeed, being allowed to do uninterrupted work is of paramount importance when it comes to developing effective study skills. Make family or housemates aware of your study hours and ask that they not disturb you. Make a schedule and hang it on the fridge or the door of your room.

# Principle #30

## Make flash cards.

Flash cards are tried and true learning tools that have helped millions of students retain information. They work because they allow your brain to drill correct answers by distilling out other nonessential information. To make a set for yourself, choose the most important facts or concepts from the material. Label the cards with a subject heading and date so you can match them with your notes or the quiz they are for. For more on flash cards, visit www.flashcardexchange. com or www.flashcardmachine.com. These sites feature flash cards on a wealth of topics and allow you to print up custom cards of your own.

# PRINCIPLE #31

## Develop a homework schedule.

Some homework takes only an hour to complete but other projects can take weeks or even the course of a whole semester. To stay on top of ongoing projects such as a paper or presentation, break down what needs to be done week by week by developing a homework schedule. Let's say you have 10 weeks to write a 20-page paper. To meet the deadline, you will need to research and write at least 2 pages per week. Two pages per week becomes your minimum milestone. You must meet this quota every week. If at any point you fail to meet your milestone, you must make up the missed time in order to stay with your schedule.

# Principle #32

## Embrace your least favorite homework.

———————————— ✴ ————————————

Every student has subjects they love and ones they dislike. You must learn to embrace even the subjects you least enjoy if you are to excel at school. Too many students only focus on the work they like because it seems fun, easy, and enjoyable. As sports coach Duke Snider has put it, "What a player does best, he should practice least. Practice is for problems." Be prepared to tackle your least favorite subjects every time you do study. As you get better at those subjects, you probably won't dislike them as much. Make it a rule to complete your least favorite homework first, when you have the most energy and attention. Then, reward yourself with your favorite subject.

# PRINCIPLE #33

## Treat homework like practice for the big game.

If school were an athletic competition, homework sessions would be practice, and tests the big game. In sports, practice is the time where you slow things down a notch and drill to perfect your throw, kick, or play. It is time spent building skills that will make you an excellent player down the road. Your homework time should follow the same logic. Don't rush through homework — use it as an opportunity to build skills you will test later. Be thorough, have patience, and practice in smaller bits. By the time you reach an important test, you will feel prepared and more at ease putting the skills learned from homework to use.

# Principle #34

## Know the point of your assignment.

Do you know why you have been given an assignment? If not, you won't get much out of it. Teachers rarely assign busy work that is unrelated to the curriculum. If you understand the purpose of your assignment and how it fits into the class, you will have an easier time doing your homework. You should be able to sum up assignments in one sentence, such as, "These exercises will help me practice adding fractions," or "Outlining this chapter will help me learn to write my own papers." If you are unable to sum it up, ask your teacher to put the assignment in context for you.

# Principle #35

## Double-check and proof your work.

Unlike timed essays or tests, homework can be perfected and polished. Make sure you turn in homework that is as error-free as possible. This means taking your time with it, double-checking to make sure you did not make a careless mistake. It also means spell-checking and catching careless grammatical errors. Many teachers take points off for sloppy or error-ridden homework. Furthermore, students who take time to double-check and proofread their homework are less likely to make errors on tests, where it counts. Spend at least 15 minutes per homework assignment, report, paper, or other project proofing your work.

# Principle #36

## Look up anything you don't know.

Because homework is not a test, you have the advantage of being able to take your time with it. Use this time to add to your body of knowledge. If you are reading a chapter and don't understand a word, take the time to look it up. If a person is referenced and you don't know who he or she is, investigate further. Desktop references such as encyclopedias, dictionaries, almanacs, and thesauruses are a great way to find factually correct information at a glance. If you take the time to look something up while doing homework, you will maximize your learning potential.

# PRINCIPLE #37

## Determine the times when you study most efficiently.

Developing good study skills means doing your homework during the times when you are most effective. It won't do you any good to read for an hour if you're feeling sleepy. Your hunger, mood, and energy level should play a role in your study habits, so don't study after a big meal, right before bed, or after a long sports practice, for instance. Also, if you're feeling stressed out, you probably won't retain as much information, so take a short break to relax and you'll be more effective. Once you've determined the times when you work efficiently, you can make the most of homework and study time.

# Principle #38

## Form a study group.

As the old saying goes, "Two heads are better than one." Double, triple, or quadruple your brainpower by forming a study group with a few classmates. When you study with others, you can take advantage of notes, skills, talents, and ideas that may be different from yours. Furthermore, explaining material to others is an excellent way to reinforce it in your own mind. The best study groups help students master material by forcing them to explain, defend, and figure out the material together. Make the most of your study group by studying on your own before meeting with the group so you come prepared with both knowledge to offer and questions to ask.

# PRINCIPLE #39

## Reward yourself!

Many students find a carrot-and-stick system of rewards very motivating for completing their homework assignments. For every chapter you read or math section you complete, reward yourself with small, satisfying breaks. Watch a little TV, check your email, noodle on the guitar, eat a healthy snack, or take your dog for a walk. Don't let these breaks turn into full-fledged distractions, however. Also, only reward yourself when you have gotten to the end of a section to maintain continuity in your thought process. Rewards help break up homework time and give you bright spots to look forward to — and they feel great when you know you have truly earned them.

# Researching, Writing, & Communicating Effectively

No student will be able to advance academically without mastering the communication skills essential to education: reading, researching, and writing. Yet American students consistently struggle with communication-related tasks such as critical-reading exercises, reading-comprehension questions, 5-paragraph essays, and research-intensive papers.

Why do students have so many problems learning to communicate effectively? In 2003, the National Commission on Writing in America's Schools and Colleges sought to find an answer to this question. After months of study, the commission, made up of teachers, school administrators, business leaders, and college and university presidents, came to some pretty disturbing conclusions about the state of reading and writing in American schools. They found that the majority of fourth-grade students spend less than 3 hours a week writing, and that nearly 66 percent of high school seniors write a 3-page paper less than once a month for their English class. Worse, 75 percent of high school seniors never receive a writing assignment in their social studies or history classes. In addition, it appears that more than 50 percent of first-year college students are incapable of submitting error-free papers. These findings led the commission to conclude in their final report, titled "The Neglected 'R': The Need for a Writing Revolution," that "despite the best efforts of many educators, writing has not received the full attention it deserves."

Unfortunately, these findings come at a time when communicating effectively is more important than ever for students seeking to advance to college and beyond. Colleges demand an increasing level of writing proficiency from incoming students, including requiring at least 1 and sometimes as many as 3 essays or writing samples to be considered for admission. The SAT test, which most college-bound students need to score well on, began requiring an essay for the first time in 2005. In addition, most college courses are writing-intensive, and students who are unable to critically read, research, and write responses, reports, and other types of papers will be unable to advance academically. The Commission's Vice-Chair Arlene Ackerman, a superintendent of schools in San Francisco, recognized the importance of strong communication skills in students when she said, "Writing is how we can teach students complex skills of synthesis, analysis, and problem solving. These skills will serve them well throughout life."

For this reason, you must master the arts of reading, researching, and writing if you hope to succeed in school and beyond. The following simple principles provide advice for how to critically read difficult pieces of text and analyze the information contained therein. You will also learn the basics of good researching and writing that you can use to craft successful papers.

# Principle #40

## Know the answers to the 6 W's.

There are 6 basic questions you should know the answers to after reading any book, article, pamphlet, short story, or other assignment. You should be able to answer questions on *who* the reading is about, *what* happened, *why* it happened, *where* it took place, *when* it occurred, and *how* an event unfolded. These questions, or the 6 W's as they are known in journalism, will get to the heart of any piece of text you are assigned to read. If you know the answers to each of these questions, you have read the text thoroughly and will be able to participate in most discussions about it.

# Principle #41

## Learn to summarize and paraphrase.

Good readers absorb what they read well enough to write about it. Sharpen your reading and writing skills by learning how to summarize or paraphrase material. Summarizing means writing a shortened version of a piece of text. Paraphrasing means rewriting a piece of text using different and fewer words that still get the main point across. Practice summarizing and paraphrasing the material you read by writing 1 summarized or paraphrased paragraph for every 3 to 5 pages of text. Your paragraph should capture the most important points that were made. Learning the art of summarizing and paraphrasing will help you understand difficult reading assignments by forcing you to explain what you read.

# PRINCIPLE #42

## Always read the introduction of the book.

Students tend to avoid reading book introductions because it seems like unnecessary work; why add extra pages to an already long reading assignment? But reading a book's introduction can actually be a shortcut in the reading process. Authors use introductions to discuss what the book is about and often provide a chapter-by-chapter review of what is to be covered. By skipping the introduction, you begin the book blindly, making it much harder to follow the author's train of thought. Reading a book's introduction, on the other hand, will give you a preview of the material to come and a leg up on those who skip it.

# Principle #43

## Get in the habit of marking up text.

If you own the book or article you are reading, get in the habit of marking it up. Research shows that active, intensive marking of text — such as highlighting, underlining, and making notes in the margins — helps improve a reader's comprehension and memory of the material. Underline passages that seem critical to you. Scribble questions or comments in the margin. These notes will be invaluable later when you need material for a paper or class comment. Be careful not to over-mark text, however; you don't want to end up with an entirely marked document. This defeats the purpose of selecting key pieces of text to stand out.

# PRINCIPLE #44

## Learn to anticipate the next step in an argument.

A good way to sharpen your critical-reading skills on non-fiction texts is to try and predict an author's next point. Every few pages, put the text down. Evaluate what the author has said thus far. What point do they appear to have laid the groundwork for? What idea might logically fit with other points they have made? By predicting what comes next in an argument you can familiarize yourself with how arguments are made and what types of evidence support them. These skills will help you better understand the material you are assigned to read and help you make logical and progressive arguments in your own papers.

# Principle #45

## Analyze or evaluate what you read.

Critical reading is when you analyze or evaluate whether a piece of text is accurate, biased, or poorly argued. You can practice your critical-reading skills on a simple editorial found in the newspaper. If the editorial is pro a certain issue, try and think of a con. If the editorial establishes a rule, think of instances in which the rule does not apply. Other things to consider when reading critically are who wrote the piece, or who published it. Is the author biased? Does the publisher or whomever funded the piece have something to gain? Examine the evidence that was used. Does it come from credible sources?

# PRINCIPLE #46

## Know how to use the library for research.

At some point, you will need to do research for a paper or extended project. Researching is an art honed over many years and entire college courses are devoted to teaching research methods. The first rule of researching is to know where to look for information. The library is the best place to find books, articles, and primary sources relating to your topic. Look at book and article titles to see if they fit your topic. Examine chapter titles and indexes to see if they contain useful information. Explore what primary sources your library has on hand — many have old newspapers and magazines on microfiche or digitally preserved.

# Principle #47

## Know how to use the Internet for research.

There are billions of pages on the Internet, but only a small fraction of them contain credible material. It is important to know how to search to yield academic research. No matter the search engine — Google, Yahoo, Ask.com, etc. — there are basic rules to Internet research. To perform targeted searches, put quotes around a word, phrase, or question you want information on. Be as specific as possible. For example, if you are researching a paper on the Battle of Bunker Hill, try typing "'Battle of Bunker Hill'+American Revolution" into the query bar. When you find material, evaluate whether it is from a trustworthy source.

# PRINCIPLE #48

## Be wary of research collected from the Web.

The Internet has revolutionized how we research. But because anyone can put information on the Internet, there is as much bad information as good. Before using research from a Web source, determine if the source is credible. Is the author or Website sponsored by a legitimate organization? Is it from a government source? Does the author have any special knowledge or training related to the topic you are researching? The best Web-based research is done via subscription-only search engines available through your library's computer network, such as InfoTrac, ProQuest, or Questia. These databases contain articles published and written by credible sources.

# Principle #49

## Never plagiarize.

Plagiarism is a very serious crime in which a student takes someone else's words or ideas and presents them as his or her own. Most schools have a policy in which any student caught plagiarizing will receive an automatic F, and some students might even be eligible for suspension. When researching and writing, be sure to keep material that you did not write yourself clearly marked as such! Put any quoted text within quotation marks. When discussing ideas you did not think of, give credit to their original source. If you do not give credit where you should, you are stealing someone else's work and will probably be punished accordingly.

# Principle #50

## Learn the components of the 5-paragraph essay.

The 5-paragraph essay discusses or analyzes one topic and is commonly used for homework assignments, in-class writing prompts, and tests. Every 5-paragraph essay begins with an introduction that expresses the main point or argument of the essay. Next come 3 supporting paragraphs, which present evidence that supports the essay's main argument. Finally, the essay ends with a conclusion that ties together what has been presented. The more comfortable you are with the components of the 5-paragraph essay, the more success you will have in school, especially on standardized tests that require them. Visit www.essayinfo.com for more information.

# Principle #51

## Learn the 6 basic essay types.

There are 6 basic formats students typically use to write essays: persuasive, expository, descriptive, narrative, cause-effect, and compare-contrast. Persuasive essays convince a reader of a point of view. Expository essays explain material in a neutral or informational way. Descriptive and narrative essays typically tell stories that feature many details. Cause-effect essays explain causes and effects of initiatives or events. Compare-contrast essays show the similarities or differences between multiple subjects. Learn which essay type applies to your topic. For example, use compare-contrast to write a paper on whether nuclear power or oil is a better fuel. For more information on these and other types of essays, visit www.essayinfo.com.

# Principle #52

## Practice writing thesis statements.

Most essays feature a thesis statement, or a single sentence that tightly and clearly presents the argument or point the author is making about a topic. The thesis statement is usually found in an essay's introduction and should clearly tell the reader what the essay will be about. A focused thesis statement also helps determine what will be in the body of an essay, because the subsequent support paragraphs are spent developing and supporting its argument. Knowing how to craft solid thesis statements will ensure your writing will be clear, well-received, and worthy of an A.

# Principle #53

## Support your essay points with appropriate pieces of evidence.

Support any arguments or assertions you make in the body of your essay with facts, details, anecdotes, examples, statistics, or quotes. For example, say you write a paper on animal testing. Your grade will suffer if you simply state that animal testing is wrong because it seems mean. An A paper will support that assertion with quotes from experts that show why animal testing is inhumane. It will explain the process of animal testing so the reader can visualize its cruelties. It will offer statistics from credible sources — for example, a government study showing most animals involved in tests suffer pain.

# Principle #54

## Always cite your sources.

You will probably need to cite your essay's sources, either using footnotes, endnotes, a works cited list, or bibliography that appears at the end of your paper. Cited sources are materials that you directly quoted from, relied heavily on, or otherwise consulted while writing. There are several different ways to structure these references, but usually the minimum amount of information you will need to provide is the author's name, the title of the article, the name of the publication it appeared in, and the date of publication. If you are confused about what information you need to list, ask your teacher. When doing your research, be sure to jot this information down so you don't have to backtrack for it later.

# GETTING READY FOR AN EXAM

If you are like many students, the very mention of a quiz, test, or exam makes your heart race. In fact, researchers estimate that between 20 and 30 percent of American students experience high or severe anxiety before tests and exams. This causes them to worry about failing; feel pessimistic about their performance even if they have studied; experience heart palpitations; feel numb or ill; forget information; sweat; tremble; and otherwise panic before and during tests. Test-taking anxiety has been cited as a major factor that prevents good students from passing basic standardized tests and explains why many students perform poorly on tests but score well on homework that covers the same material.

Interestingly, studies show that both good and bad students feel equally anxious about taking tests. Whether they have prepared or not prepared for a test usually makes little difference in students' anxiety. Instead, the single greatest contributing factor to a student's test-taking anxiety is their dislike of being scrutinized. The feeling of being studied, put on the spot, timed, or otherwise having their knowledge closely monitored leaves both good and bad students feeling claustrophobic. Minimizing anxiety over exams, therefore, can be achieved by learning to feel more comfortable being scrutinized.

Of course, the biggest way to minimize anxiety over exams is to be well-prepared for them. Being prepared means making sure you know the information inside out and up and down. But there are other ways to mentally, emotionally and physically prepare for exams that will reduce the amount of anxiety you feel over tests. These include getting a good night's sleep, avoiding cramming, eating healthy foods, and having the self-confidence to know you can pass. The following simple principles contain these and other tips, tricks, and ideas that will help all students get ready for tests, and perform their best on them.

# PRINCIPLE #55

## Find out the format of the test.

Very rarely do teachers fail to give any hints about what form a test will take. They will usually let you know whether their test features multiple-choice, true-or-false, fill-in-the-blank, and/or essay questions. Once you know the format of the test, you can focus your test preparation in those areas. For example, multiple-choice and true-false questions tend to judge factual and reading-comprehension knowledge. Essay-based tests, on the other hand, test a student's ability to outline, craft, and sustain an argument. Knowing the format of the test beforehand will help you prepare most effectively.

# PRINCIPLE #56

## Condense the information.

At heart, studying for a test is about reviewing information you have already learned and condensing it into smaller and smaller pieces. To do this, summarize your notes by making outlines of them. The outline should contain the major ideas that will trigger other thoughts and information stored in your brain. Re-outline until all the essential information fits on one page. Another way to condense information is to make flash cards. Put a definition, historical event, or math formula on one side of the card. On the other, put a trigger word that will remind you of the rest of the information. Condensing information into progressively smaller pieces makes studying more manageable and effective.

# Principle #57

## Avoid pulling an all-nighter.

---- ✳ ----

Successful students know that getting enough sleep is directly tied to superior academic performance. Getting a good night's sleep before a test is especially important. While some students are tempted to pull an all-nighter as a last-ditch effort to learn the material, research shows that not sleeping before a test will probably lead you to do poorly on it. A study by University of Virginia scientists found that sleep-deprived students score, on average, 7 points lower than well-rested ones. Said Paul Suratt, head researcher, "Sleep disorders can impair children's I.Q.s as much as lead exposure." Be sure to get a good night's sleep before your test so you score your best.

# Principle #58

## Avoid cramming.

---

※

---

Cramming, or learning a subject shortly before you are to be tested, is not a recommended study method. Cramming forces your brain to store information in your short-term memory, where it is quickly forgotten. While cramming may help you remember a few additional vocabulary words or history dates, it does not allow you to form lasting connections to the material. Studying regularly, on the other hand, lets your brain store information in your long-term memory, leaving you with knowledge you can use over time. As the philosopher William James put it, "Cramming seeks to stamp things in by intense application immediately before the ordeal. But a thing thus learned can form but few associations."

# PRINCIPLE #59

## Eat a healthy breakfast.

Ever wonder why breakfast has been labeled the most important meal of the day? The answer is simple. When you sleep, you engage in an 8- to 10-hour fast, which causes your metabolism to slow. When your cells do not receive sufficient nutrition immediately following the fast, they fail to function as efficiently. For this reason, people who skip breakfast are more likely to be tired, clumsy, distracted, and unfocused. None of these are traits you want on test day! To score your best, eat a healthy, nutritious breakfast. Also, if permitted, bring a snack to munch on in case you get hungry during the exam.

# Principle #60

## Dress for the test.

Tests are not fashion shows, so don't show up dressed for one! It is important to dress comfortably on the day of the test. This means wearing clothes that are not too tight, that you can shift positions easily in, and that you feel your best in. It is a good idea to dress in layers. This way, if the exam room is too warm or cool, you will be able to peel off or put on an extra layer. Above all, wear clothes that will not make you feel self-conscious. You don't need to be worrying if your neighbor can see your underwear while conjugating verbs or diagramming sentences.

# Principle #61

## Attend review sessions.

Teachers commonly offer review sessions, especially prior to big exams. During them, teachers review what material is likely to appear on the test, what format it might appear in, and help students with especially difficult pieces of the material. Review sessions are a fantastic opportunity to prepare for a test, yet the majority of students fail to take advantage of these exceptional forums. Data from one New York City public school showed that just 8 percent of 10th-graders attended review sessions offered by their teachers. Always attend review sessions, or, ask your teachers to consider offering one if they don't already.

# Principle #62

## Form a test-specific study group.

Get together with a group of study partners within 48 hours of any test. Forming a test-specific study group allows you to take advantage of others' notes and knowledge of the information on which you are to be tested. When you study with others, you can get answers to questions you can't answer yourself. You can also reinforce your grasp on a subject by explaining it to others. For inspiration, share with the group the following advice from basketball coach Pat Riley: "There can only be one state of mind as you approach any profound test; total concentration, a spirit of togetherness, and strength."

# Principle #63

## Make up possible test questions.

An excellent way to study for an exam is to generate questions you think might be on the test. Doing this helps you study in 2 ways. First, it forces you to review all material from the teacher's perspective. In doing so you will get inside your teacher's head and come face to face with material you, the student, may have overlooked. Second, you can practice answering these questions, which will greatly prepare you if they actually end up being on the test. For maximum results, find a study partner and encourage him or her to make up test questions you can exchange.

# PRINCIPLE #64

## Learn the correct answers to questions missed on previous exams.

——————— ✳ ———————

When studying, go over all previous tests and quizzes. There is information in them that can affect your score on the upcoming exam. Look closely at questions you missed. Did you not know the information? Do you know it now? Did the format of the question confuse you? Is the teacher likely to use it again? Learning the correct answers ensures you will not make the same error twice. As author Dale E. Turner wisely noted, "Some of the best lessons we ever learn are learned from past mistakes. The error of the past is the wisdom and success of the future."

# PRINCIPLE #65

## Believe you can do it!

Your educational success hinges on your ability to think positively about yourself. Believing you can advance academically and succeed in the face of a challenge is an important part of accomplishing both goals. Instead of thinking, "I will never pass this test," tell yourself that anything is possible if you are willing to work for it. As psychology professor and educational expert Carol Dweck says, "Study skills and learning skills are inert until they're powered by an active ingredient." That active ingredient, according to Dweck, is the belief that you will succeed. "If you target that belief," says Dweck, "you can see more benefit than you have any reason to hope for."

# Taking Tests

It is often said that tests do not measure what a person truly knows, only how well he or she takes tests. While that may be true, tests are, more than ever, an integral part of education. Since the passage of the educational act known as No Child Left Behind, standardized tests are a required and possibly permanent feature of every school in the United States. Furthermore, all 4-year colleges and universities, and many 2-year colleges, require students to pass college entrance exams, such as the SAT or ACT tests, simply to be considered for admission. So while tests may only measure how good you are at taking tests, if you can become a great test-taker, you are sure to excel at school.

In many ways, taking a test is like playing a game. You have to know the rules and abide by them. You also may be able to learn certain tricks to help you out in a jam or give you the edge over others. Educational consultants James J. Messina,

Ph.D. and Constance M. Messina, Ph.D, advise students to "consider the test a contest — you versus the test-maker." Indeed, you can prepare for this contest the same way you would prepare for a sports match or musical competition: by practicing.

If you find you are a habitually weak test-taker, make sure you excel in other areas of your academic portfolio, such as class participation, homework completion, and essay writing. Also, if you are concerned you may have a learning disorder that impedes your ability to perform your best on tests, discuss the possibility of getting evaluated by a specialist with your parents and teachers. These students can be granted permission to take untimed tests or use special study guides while they are tested. These are only offered to students who have been diagnosed with serious learning disorders, however, and are not meant to be abused by lazy students who don't feel like studying.

To maximize your chances of passing tests, study the following simple principles. They will help you approach any exam with confidence, calm, and clarity.

# PRINCIPLE #66

## Arrive early for tests.

Showing up to a test even 1 minute late will hurt your ability to maximize your grade. If you rush into your seat as the bell rings and are fumbling to get organized, you will start the test flustered and out-of-sorts. Furthermore, rushing causes you to forget critical items, such as extra pencils, pens, or the proper calculator. To get the best grade, always arrive to a test on time — or better yet, get there 15 minutes early to collect your thoughts and go over your notes. If the test is at a site that is unfamiliar to you (as many college-entrance exams are) be sure you have directions to the testing center in advance, and know to which room you must report.

# Principle #67

## Bring the right equipment.

Many tests require that you bring certain supplemental items, such as a No. 2 pencil, ruler, or a calculator. Read all testing literature in advance to find out exactly what materials you need. Some math tests, for example, require a graphing calculator; others forbid graphing calculators because of their ability to store formulas. Bringing the wrong kind of calculator could force you to forfeit your ability to use one during the test, which will make it difficult for you to pass. Pack these materials in advance of the test, and bring a backup set in case your pencil breaks or your calculator battery dies.

# Principle #68

## Take a few deep breaths before and during the test.

Breathing deeply reduces stress and promotes clear thinking. Prior to and during a test, take a few deep breaths that start low in your belly. Exhale until every bit of air has left your lungs. This type of breathing fills the lungs' air pockets, allowing you to take in more oxygen and release more carbon dioxide. The end result is more oxygen flowing to your brain and lymphatic systems, which releases endorphins, the body's natural relaxants. When you are stressed, deep breathing will ease you into a state of physical calm and clarity, the ideal state for taking a test.

# PRINCIPLE #69

## Scan the entire test before you start.

Don't discover what is on a test page by page. Your very first action after the test begins should be to scan the entire test. Become familiar with the test's contents right away. This will help you budget your time and approach the test as a whole, with confidence and clarity. Remember, you usually don't have to take the test in the order it appears. Start with the sections you know best. These will take you the least amount of time, leaving more time to spend on harder sections. Also, sometimes questions have their answers in other areas of the test, and you can find these by scanning the test before you begin working.

# Principle #70

## Read test directions carefully.

---- ✳ ----

Countless test-takers have had their hard work go to waste because they failed to read test directions. They work in pencil when the test requires pen; they write an essay that argues against the example when the directions are to argue in favor of it. Reduce your chance of making such mistakes by reading the test's direction before you begin your work. Also, never assume that the first set of directions applies to the entire test. While the first section of the test may have wanted you to pick the answer *most* like the example, the second section may want you to pick the answer *least* like the example. Prevent yourself from making this mistake by looking for new sets of directions that may appear at a new section of the test.

# Principle #71

## Always show your work.

When taking math or science exams, make sure to show how you arrived at your answer by documenting every step. Too often, careless mistakes are made because students add in their head or divide on the fly. Showing your work will cut down on accidental errors you might make on your test. Also, showing your work can help you get partial credit. Even if your answer is wrong, most teachers will give partial credit if you had the process correct up until the point at which you made the mistake. Finally, showing your work eliminates any question of whether you cheated, which can come in handy should you be accused.

# PRINCIPLE #72

## Make a plan of attack.

After you scan the test and familiarize yourself with its contents, take 30 seconds to plan how you will attack each section. This will prevent you from running out of time or spending too much time on the wrong parts of the test. Budget your time based on the make-up of the test. Essay questions, for example, always take longer than multiple choice. If your test features both, make sure you leave enough time to write the essay. Sometimes, teachers list how many points certain sections of the test are worth. In this case, budget your time to spend the most time on the questions that are worth the most points.

# Principle #73

## Recognize that blank answers are always wrong.

Never leave a test question blank — if you don't answer, you have no chance at earning points for it. If the question is multiple choice, the answer is right in front of you. Eliminate the answers you know are wrong and guess from the remaining answers. For fill-in-the-blank questions, write an answer that could be correct — better to get it wrong because you tried than because you left it blank. (It is important to note that on the SAT and PSAT, 1/4 of a point is deducted for wrong answers and nothing is deducted for blank answers. So, if you can't make an educated guess at an SAT question, it is actually in your favor to skip it and leave it blank.)

# Principle #74

## Go with your gut.

Self-doubt can be your worst enemy during quiz time. If you are stuck, go with your gut: research show your first guess is probably correct. A 2007 study from University College London found that people are more likely to perform well if they trust their instincts rather than laboring over a decision. The study, published in the journal *Current Biology*, concluded that in some cases, instinctual decisions are more reliable than decisions made using more involved cognitive processes. So stick with the response your gut tells you is right, even if you aren't sure why your instinct points you toward that answer. As American essayist Ralph Waldo Emerson wrote, "Trust the instinct to the end, though you can render no reason."

# Principle #75

## Let the test's language be your guide.

— ✳ —

If you are stumped, use the test's language to your advantage. Certain wordings can be red flags that tell you an answer is not correct, or if you should answer the question in a particular way. True-false questions that contain absolute words such as "never," "always," "all," and "none" are likely to be false. The right answer will probably contain more reasonable words such as "usually," "generally," and "often." Also, look for words that help you figure out what the question wants you to do. For example, "if" statements usually have a "then" counterpart — focus your answer on explaining that counterpart. Let the test's language naturally guide you toward the right answers.

# Principle #76

## Be neat.

---

It may seem petty, but many teachers take off points for sloppy or illegible work. Therefore, write as neatly as possible. On essay questions, make sure every word you write is legible. If you can't read your own handwriting, whoever grades your test certainly won't be able to. Avoid losing points because someone couldn't decipher your words. If the test is a math exam, make sure your work is neat and orderly. Keep numbers in columns. Make sure the steps you went through to derive your answer are clearly readable to your teacher.

# Principle #77

## Use all the time allotted for a test.

Never turn in a test early — use any remaining time to proofread your work. Double-check the math you've done; proofread an essay for spelling errors and grammatical mistakes. Teachers report that students perform markedly better when they take the time to check their work. Says one long-time teacher, Jordan McMullin, "I can't tell you how many students lose needless points because they don't take the time to check their work. I'd have to say that students who proofread their work score on average 10 points higher than those who do not."

# Principle #78

## Learn from your mistakes.

Rarely do students score 100 percent on an exam. You probably will make at least a few mistakes on a test, and that's OK. Learn from these mistakes to improve for the next one. When you get a test back, go over it carefully. Look at the kinds of mistakes you made. Examine the areas in which you were weak. Did you rush? Make careless errors? Not know the information? Most important, find out what the correct answers are and study them for next time. Making a mistake once is acceptable, but not twice. As the old Chinese proverb says, "Fool me once, shame on you; fool me twice, shame on me."

# Being Responsible

There is perhaps nothing that recoils the average student more than a reminder to "be responsible." Upon simply hearing the phrase, most students groan, protest, or at the very least, roll their eyes and make a face. Rather than lecturing students on the importance of becoming a responsible person, it is perhaps more effective to show an example of what happens when a student fails to develop responsibility.

Consider this example: "Rob," a high school freshman, like many students, was not the model of responsibility. He turned homework in late; he lost track of test dates and thus failed to study properly. Once, he cheated on a final paper and was forced to take a zero in the class, bringing his already-low grade point average down so significantly that he was unable to get into the college of his choice.

Rob did go to college, however, and was excited to be there.

He was finally free from the rules and parameters of high school! But Rob quickly found that without a strict schedule and enforced rules, there was nothing to keep him on track in college. Because he was not as responsible as other college students, he had a difficult time managing the freedom of the university environment. Without a school bell reminding him where he needed to be, he showed up late for class. He also had a hard time saying no to social engagements, and thus his studies suffered. By the time he was able to discipline himself, 2 years of college had passed and he was near the bottom of the class. Rob eventually graduated, but did not earn good enough grades to be offered the kinds of top jobs his classmates were getting. He finally did land a job, but quickly became known as an average, irresponsible employee.

Rob's main problem is that he never learned to be responsible. He failed to develop a few basic skills that people need to succeed in high school, college, and elsewhere in life. You can protect yourself against a similar fate by integrating the following simple principles for being responsible into your academic routine.

# PRINCIPLE #79

## Turn in all assignments on time.

— ✳ —

It should go without saying that all homework, reports, and other assignments must be turned in on time. Work received late is usually not eligible for full credit. Most teachers deduct a certain number of points or a whole grade for every day an assignment is late. For full credit, aim to turn your work in on time, or better yet, early. Some teachers will review work turned in early and allow you to fix mistakes at no consequence to your grade.

# Principle #80

## Ask for extensions only when you really need them.

Everyone knows the story of the boy who cried wolf: he set off so many false alarms that no one believed him when he was telling the truth. Avoid becoming the student who cried wolf by only asking for extensions when you truly need them. Asking for too many extensions gives teachers the impression you are a lazy, disorganized student more interested in dreaming up elaborate excuses than doing your work. Furthermore, should something happen that causes you to really need an extension, your teacher may not grant it, based on your reputation.

# PRINCIPLE #81

## Be a student with integrity.

Hard, honest work shows. So does laziness. It is true that many schools are competitive places, and some students reach success by thwarting or sabotaging other students. But realize you can never truly succeed in school, or in the real world, if you take malicious shortcuts. You might find short-term success, but you will also give yourself the reputation of being careless, manipulative, or a liar. As legendary college football coach Joe Paterno once noted, "Success without honor is an unseasoned dish; it will satisfy your hunger, but it won't taste good." There is no solid academic future for the student who feels compelled to deceive to get ahead in school.

# PRINCIPLE #82

## Recognize that being wrong is part of learning.

When you give the wrong answer in class, how do you react? Do you pause, and calmly seek out the correct answer? Or do you cop an attitude and blame a third party? Unfortunately, most students do the latter. Being unable to accept that they are wrong is difficult for immature students who are still learning how to be responsible young adults. Successful students realize that everyone is wrong sometimes — and this time it might be you. Don't be embarrassed when you are wrong. Instead, gracefully take responsibility for your mistakes and learn the correct answer for next time.

# Principle #83

## Come to class every day.

---- ❋ ----

It might be tempting to skip class from time to time, but coming to classes, meetings, and other activities every day demonstrates your respect for your teachers and fellow students. When students ditch class, they miss important notes, dates, and information, and waste the time of the teacher and fellow learners. If you never skip class you will avoid feeling unfocused or flustered because you aren't up to date on lecture material. As Woody Allen once quipped, "Eighty percent of success is showing up." Show those you go to school with that you value their time and efforts by coming to class every day.

# Principle #84

## Never cheat.

Recent surveys have found that an alarming number of students cheat at some point in their educational career. A 2002 study of students nationwide found that 75 percent of them had cheated; another study found that 100 percent of teachers polled had caught students cheating. Cheating has obvious consequences, such as earning an F, being suspended, and the incident going on your permanent record. But less obvious are the damages to a student's confidence, honor, and pride. As the classic playwright Sophocles said, "I would prefer even to fail with honor than to win by cheating." Keep your academic performance something you can be proud of by never cheating.

# PRINCIPLE #85

## Avoid socializing in class.

Although your friends may all be gathered together in the same room, class is not a party, and never the time to socialize. Being respectful and creating an environment in which you and others can learn means refraining from turning the classroom into social hour. Avoid being chatty with friends during lessons or group projects. Keep your energy focused on the lecture or project at hand. Above all, never pass notes or send text message in class. According to a 2007 survey, more than 70 percent of students admitted to text messaging while in class! Responsible students save texting and other forms of socializing for lunch hour, before or after school, or weekends.

# PRINCIPLE #86

## Never copy, buy, or steal work found on the Internet.

The Internet has revolutionized the way students learn. However, it has also revolutionized their ability to plagiarize. A 2002 national survey of high school students found more than half had plagiarized content from the Web. And while the Internet has offered students the opportunity to cheat, it has also offered teachers opportunities to better catch them. Many have access to Websites and databases that crosscheck work for mass production or previous publication. Your teachers know your writing style and it will be quite obvious should you attempt to pass off someone else's work as your own. Take the time to do your own research and writing.

# Principle #87

## Respect your teachers.

Academic Donald D. Quinn famously said, "If a doctor, lawyer, or dentist had 40 people in his office at one time, all of whom had different needs, and some of whom didn't want to be there and were causing trouble, and [they] had to treat them all with professional excellence for 9 months, then he might have some conception of the classroom teacher's job." Not only is teaching difficult, but it is often underpaid; the National Education Association says making ends meet on a teacher's salary is so hard that nearly half quit within 5 years. Those who stay do so because they love it. Respect your teachers for committing their lives to enriching your future.

# Principle #88

## Start an assignment calendar — and use it.

Keep track of all assignments, deadlines, and test dates by keeping a calendar or dayplanner. The minute a new test, project, or homework is assigned, write it down! Be sure to block out enough time to work on an assignment or study for a quiz. Make time each day to review the week's upcoming workload so there are no surprises. In addition to helping you stay organized for the future, an assignment calendar helps you keep track of what you've done in the past. It is also useful to look back at it throughout the semester to remind yourself of what you've accomplished.

# Principle #89

## Learn to say "no" when you are too busy to hang out.

Perhaps the hardest part of becoming a responsible student is learning when to sacrifice your social life for studying. There will be times when, in the name of responsibility, you have to turn down a friend's invitation to see a movie or attend a party because you need to hit the books. Counteract this reality by making sure to do something social at least 3 times a week. Put these dates on your academic calendar and look forward to them as rewards for being a hardworking, responsible student who knows that studying comes before socializing.

# MANAGING YOUR TIME

An old saying goes, "To know where you can find something is the chief part of learning." Indeed, being organized and managing your time is at the heart of being a successful student, and is the foundation from which many other good academic habits spring. Managing your time helps a student avoid feeling stressed and under-prepared, which, in turn, improves productivity, focus, and concentration. Likewise, being organized helps a student feel in control, which heralds self-confidence.

Why do so many students have difficulty managing their time? The answer largely lies in technology. While certain technological advancements have benefited students' ability to perform in school, other devices have eroded their ability to concentrate on one task at a time, serving as distractions of epic proportion. While the Internet and other high-tech devices commonly carried by students, such as cell phones or personal digital assistants (PDAs), have allowed them to take care of homework and fact-finding more efficiently, they have also opened up a Pandora's box of social networking opportunities. Indeed, students of the 21st century email, IM, and text message each other almost nonstop. The Internet is laden with distracting sites such as MySpace, Facebook, and YouTube, which can quickly derail a student with the best plans for studying. The fast-paced, instant gratification quality of the information age has also cut down on students' ability to focus on one task until it is complete and has encouraged them to replace productivity with sociability. Thus, many students end up using these technological marvels for social ends, rather than academic ones.

In reality, there is no magic trick to learning how to manage your time. All it takes is the will to create good systems, the resolution to stick with them, and the self-discipline to say "no" to distractions that will derail you from your studies. By integrating the following principles into your life, you will learn how to manage your time for a successful academic career.

# Principle #90

## Break work down into smaller bits.

Make a big project or daunting assignment seem more approachable by breaking it down into bite-sized tasks. Make a list with the task you ultimately need to accomplish at the top. Then outline each step involved in accomplishing the project. Put a line through each entry as you complete steps. Before you know it, you will have completed the assignment and all that will remain on the page is your finished project. By building a clear road map to your goal, you can avoid procrastination and reduce the overwhelming feeling of "Where do I begin?" that often accompanies large projects.

# PRINCIPLE #91

## Prioritize daily tasks.

Managing both your academic and extracurricular life can be accomplished through prioritizing daily tasks. Before you go to bed each night, make a list of things you must take care of the next day by writing them down in order of importance. Shortly after you wake up, read your list to remind yourself what you need to accomplish. Likewise, throughout the day at school, add other tasks that you must do when you get home. Keep these lists written in a small notebook you carry at all times; this way, when a task pops into your mind, you can get it down on your list before you forget.

# Principle #92

## Don't wait until the last minute.

Sometimes, the hardest part of doing homework or working on a project is just getting started. You may procrastinate because you feel overwhelmed by the task at hand; however, waiting until the last minute to complete an assignment can have unfortunate consequences. Beginning a paper the night before it is due will cause unnecessary stress. If you procrastinate, you may find a project requires more time than you had anticipated, but you won't have the extra hours. If you put off your homework until the last minute, you certainly won't be able to turn in your best work. Start early; give yourself plenty of time to map out, complete, and proof your work to make it your best and avoid feeling stressed out.

# PRINCIPLE #93

## Save time by keeping your work space organized.

An old adage says, "For every minute spent in organizing, an hour is earned." Indeed, organizing your bedroom, desk, backpack, locker, or other school-related space will save you hours of wasted time. Take a few minutes each day to put away clothes, organize papers, throw away trash, and otherwise clear your desk. Create a system for storing old notebooks and tests so you can quickly find what you need when studying for your final at the end of the semester. You'll appreciate the freshness of an organized desk when you next return to it, and will find it easier to jump right into work instead of getting derailed by preliminary tasks.

# Principle #94

## Learn how long it takes you to do homework.

Unless you know approximately how long it takes you to write a 3-page paper or do 20 algebra problems, how will you be able to leave yourself enough time to do it? Successful students monitor how long it takes them to do their work so they can plan for the future. The next time you have an assignment, keep your eyes on the clock. Did you read 20 pages of text in 45 minutes? Did it take you 4 hours to write your 5-paragraph essay? Learning how long it takes you to do your homework will allow you to precisely budget time for it every day.

# PRINCIPLE #95

## Learn your productive hours.

Everyone has different hours or days that bring out their productive side. For example, a recent survey conducted by CareerWomen.com found that Tuesdays between 10 a.m. and noon is the most productive time of week for U.S. workers. Whether it be a Tuesday morning or not, learn when your peak performance hours occur so you can make the most out of your productive zone. In general, people tend to be less productive late at night and after they have eaten large meals. Save your most intensive work for the hours when you know you are most alert and ready to learn.

# Principle #96

## Don't begin an assignment until you are truly ready to finish it.

Many students start homework but get distracted before they can finish. Maximize your time by only starting large assignments when you have time to finish them. For example, it doesn't make sense to start writing a paper 15 minutes before dinner will be ready. By the time you get into a groove, you will need to take a break! Doing large projects in segments is fine, but make sure the time you give to assignments is substantial enough to actually accomplish something. The 15 minutes before dinner are better spent on smaller tasks, such as memorizing multiplication tables or history dates.

# Principle #97

## Have frequently used items accessible at all times.

The average person wastes 6 weeks a year looking for misplaced items. To minimize the time you spend looking for things, ask yourself, "What do I use every single day?" Gather those things and keep them in your backpack, locker, or desk at home. Having to search for a calculator when you finally settle into your homework causes an unnecessary moment of distraction. Likewise, frantically searching for the padlock to your locker every time you leave for school interrupts your ability to focus on where you need to go. Managing your time means having daily items ready to go at a moment's notice.

# PRINCIPLE #98

## Make use of your free time.

Some days are so busy, it feels like every hour is booked. Yet even the busiest day contains spots of "dead time" that can be used to your academic advantage. The 20 minutes spent waiting for or riding the bus, for example, can be used to your benefit if you know how to manage your time. The work done during free time should be light, and preferably memorization-related. SAT vocabulary words, chemistry tables, or history dates are all perfect things to study during chunks of otherwise dead time. The next time you find yourself waiting for a ride, an appointment, or a game to start, whip out your study aids.

# Principle #99

## Save time to have fun every day!

No one can study all the time, and nor should they. When you are managing your time, make sure you carve out some hours in which to have fun! Spend at least an hour a day doing an activity you truly enjoy. This could be playing an instrument you love, going to sports practice, reading a fun book, spending time with your family, or just hanging out with friends after school. During this "me time," don't allow yourself to feel guilty that you could be studying or working on a project — time spent with friends or doing activities you love is never time wasted. As the Scottish writer and spiritual leader Eileen Caddy advised, "Live and work but do not forget to play, to have fun in life and really enjoy it."

# LEARNING YOUR ACADEMIC STRENGTHS & WEAKNESSES

Learning is a highly personal endeavor. Indeed, there are as many ways to learn as there are learners! If you struggle with certain aspects of school, take comfort in the fact that there is no one, right, or true way to learn something. The only "right" way of learning is the combination that complements your individual academic strengths and weaknesses — in other words, whatever works for you.

Unfortunately, due to overcrowding and underfunding, many schools have been forced to tailor their programs for the masses. Curricula are often designed with the lowest common denominator in mind, and instructors must teach to a baseline that is designed for the average student's abilities. Giving education a one-size-fits-all approach is the only realistic way to teach the 30 or even 40 students that tend to be crowded into the modern classroom. Unfortunately, this approach fails to account for the fact that students have widely ranging academic strengths and weakness. Because students learn so differently, they would be better served by an academic program tailored to their individual needs. Obviously, this is something the public education system is unable to provide. But by becoming aware of your academic strengths and weaknesses on your own, you can get closer to a personalized academic program built around your unique assets and shortcomings.

The following simple principles will help you become aware of the ways in which you learn best. Some students may balk at the idea of examining their weaknesses. They should take comfort in the fact that having both strengths and weaknesses is normal and natural. As the American writer Marge Piercy has put it, "My strength and my weakness are twins in the same womb."

With that in mind, use the following simple principles to identify your academic strengths and weaknesses and learn how to use both to excel at school.

# Principle #100

## Determine whether you are an auditory or visual learner.

The eyes and ears make powerful learning aids. Students who learn visually gain knowledge best through pictures, charts, diagrams, videos, and illustrations. Creating a picture or visual representation of material helps further cement information in their minds. Auditory learners, on the other hand, benefit from information accompanied by sounds. They best absorb material when it is paired with seminars, presentations, debates, or lectures. Try and figure out which type of learner you are by paying attention to classes in which you feel fully engaged with the material. Do these classes feature visual or auditory components? Then, seek out those types of classes.

# Principle #101

## Determine whether you are a hands-on learner.

While people learn by participating, some need to experience a lesson firsthand in order to benefit from it. If you are a hands-on or kinesthetic learner, choose projects that let you get into the nitty-gritty of a topic. Participate in science experiments; learn economics by starting a small business. Some of the world's most successful people have been hands-on learners. Consider Michael Dell, who dropped out of the University of Texas because he needed a more hands-on learning experience than lectures could provide. He started a small business selling computer parts out of his dorm room — and within 10 years was at the helm of a multimillion-dollar company.

# Principle #102

## Determine whether you are a practical learner.

Some students are easily overwhelmed by the amount of information and responsibility school requires. Consequently, they learn best in a fact-based and structured environment. If you like to make lists, do workbook assignments, learn specific examples, and work on problems that have definitive right-or-wrong answers (such as math problems), you are probably a practical learner. Practical learners excel in math and science, so you should put your energies towards these subjects. When you have the option, choose concrete, defined projects such as dioramas, exhibits, or proofs over open-ended, creative ones such as creative essays or artistic projects.

# PRINCIPLE #103

## Determine whether you are an interpretive learner.

Yet another type of learner is the student who learns in an artistic, interpretive, or emotional way. These students excel at creative writing, the arts, and production-related projects. They typically are unafraid to try new things, explore their feelings, go out on a limb, and be the center of attention. While the interpretive learner excels at artistic endeavors, they can often work their creativity into subjects across the curriculum. For example, a musical student might work music into physics class by doing a project on sound waves. The creative writer might apply his or her talents to history class by writing a piece of historical fiction for a final project.

# Principle #104

## Determine whether you are a natural researcher.

Students who are natural researchers enjoy digging for information to support their opinions, or the opinions of others. They excel at reading, non-fiction writing, debating, and researching, and tend to have good memory for facts, examples, and statistics that can be used to support a position. Natural researchers do well in research-intensive fields, particularly the hard sciences and law. They like developing ideas, analyzing information, drawing conclusions, and writing short, pertinent papers. If this sounds like you, perhaps you will agree with the famous lawyer Dudley Field Malone, who once said, "I have never in my life learned anything from any man who agreed with me."

# PRINCIPLE #105

## Determine whether you are a brainstormer.

Some students excel at out-of-the-box thinking. They perform best when faced with open-ended problems that have no wrong answers. Students who are natural brainstormers enjoy strategizing, finding alternatives, troubleshooting problems, predicting outcomes, and creating analogies. Their ability to predict and adapt to changing situations makes them poised to become entrepreneurs, politicians, and troubleshooters. It was perhaps this class of student that writer and futurist Alvin Toffler was thinking of when he said, "The illiterate of the 21st century will not be those who cannot read and write, but those who cannot learn, unlearn, and relearn."

# Principle #106

## Recognize you have a variety of academic strengths.

It is rare to find a student who perfectly matches only one of the aforementioned learning types, and even rarer to find a student who fits none. A combination of these profiles probably applies to you. Identify which ones best describe your learning strengths. Then, match assignments, projects, and in-class learning exercises to your strengths. If you determine you are a hands-on and interpretive learner, ask if you can produce an amateur film that reenacts a Civil War battle for your final history project. If you determine you are a visual and practical learner, you may want to design or engineer an apparatus for your physics or math class.

# Principle #107

## Seek out extra-credit assignments to balance out weaknesses.

It will not always be possible to blend your strengths into all topics. For example, a student who excels at writing will have difficulty applying that skill to chemistry and math class. If you are particularly weak in a subject and cannot find a way to integrate your strengths, ask your teacher for extra-credit assignments. An extra-credit project might be a book report, short paper, or to watch a film and write about it. Many times, teachers will let you propose your own extra-credit ideas. These projects not only give you the chance to improve your grade, they improve your skills by allowing you to get additional practice in subjects that are hard for you.

# Principle #108

## Learn outside the classroom.

For some students, their biggest weakness is the classroom itself. A 2007 study by Indiana University found that 2 out of every 3 students are bored in at least 1 class every day. Finding learning opportunities beyond the classroom to make your time in it more productive. Some of history's greatest minds learned best outside the classroom. As Winston Churchill said, "I am always ready to learn although I do not always like being taught." If you like social science or economics, volunteer at a shelter or intern for a business or political campaign. If you enjoy history or biology, visit a museum or aquarium. Or, in your free time, read the biography of a famous person in American history.

# PRINCIPLE #109

## Get tested for a learning disorder.

If your academic weaknesses consistently overshadow your strengths, you might suffer from a learning disorder. Learning disorders cause students to have difficulty reading, writing, speaking, learning math, or paying attention. Note that learning disorders are not mental or emotional disorders, and are unrelated to a person's race, ethnicity, or economic standing. Nearly 3 million students have been diagnosed with a learning disorder and are eligible to receive special education services under the Individuals with Disabilities Education Act (IDEA). Learning disabilities are usually identified through a series of IQ tests and neuropsychological exams. If you believe you have one, talk to your parents and teachers about getting tested.

# Maintaining Healthy Habits

In 2002, school administrators at Whitefish Central School in Montana began to notice that discipline problems among the student body seemed on the rise. Students were constantly being pulled out of the classroom and sent to the principal's office, which was interfering with learning. After carefully studying the problem, they noticed that most disruptive behaviors occurred in the afternoon, about an hour after lunch. School officials wondered: Could students' disruptive behaviors be the result of eating unhealthy foods at lunch?

To test the theory, the school restricted the number of high-fat and sugary foods offered on campus. They replaced vending machine sodas with bottled water and natural juices. All candy was eliminated from the cafeteria and vending machines. They increased offerings of healthy foods such as sandwiches, yogurt, fruit, milk, bagels, and salads. Within 2 years, school administrators were astonished to find that disciplinary referrals had fallen dramatically. Prior to the nutritional changes, about

10 to 12 students were being sent to the principal's office every day; following the nutritional changes, students were being removed from class for behavior problems at a rate of just 4 to 8 students in an entire week!

Whitefish Central School found these healthy habits had other positive benefits for learning. Teachers reported that because students were calmer, more alert and more focused, they were able to get 10 to 15 percent more teaching time into every class. The student body also began scoring better on tests, and the school's state ranking improved (it currently ranks in the 76th percentile of all schools in the state). Said Principal Kim Anderson, "There has been a tremendous change in our students' behavior since we improved our food program. … Nutrition is the missing link between academics and behavior in the classroom."

Indeed, nutritious meals are just one healthy habit that can help you excel in school. Getting enough exercise and sleep are also important for becoming a stellar student. The following principles will teach you these and other healthy habits that support learning and show you how to integrate them into your life.

# Principle #110

## Avoid becoming overweight.

Child obesity is a growing problem in America. One-third of U.S. students are overweight, and 17 percent are obese. Being overweight not only lowers students' self-confidence — it puts them at risk for weight-related diseases such as diabetes and heart disease. It also reduces their ability to excel at school. A 2003 *Journal of the American Medical Association* study found that severely overweight students were 4 times more likely than healthy students to experience impaired school functioning. Another study by the RAND Corporation found that overweight students score lower on math and reading tests than their non-overweight peers. Increase your odds of being an excellent student by keeping your weight in check.

# Principle #111

## Don't let yourself get hungry.

A growling stomach can be as bad for your academic career as an overly full one. Research shows that hungry students perform poorly in class and on exams. One study published in the *Journal of the American Academy of Child & Adolescent Psychiatry* found that hungry students were twice as likely to have impaired neural functioning and high rates of hyperactivity, absenteeism, and tardiness. Hunger that results from skipping meals or under-eating can compromise cognitive development and school performance. If you are concerned about your weight, skipping meals is not the answer. Keep nutritious snacks such as carrots, yogurt, and granola bars on hand so you can look and score your best.

# Principle #112

## Healthy eating brings the A's your way.

Eating healthy, nutritious foods provides your brain with the essential vitamins, minerals, and proteins it needs to function properly. A lack of nutrients can have disastrous consequences on your academic record. For example, students deficient in iron — found in leafy, green vegetables — tend to exhibit shortened attention span, irritability, fatigue, and difficulty concentrating. One study published in *Pediatrics* found that students who are deprived of essential nutrients have significantly lower math scores and are more likely to repeat a grade and be suspended from school. Make sure your meals and snacks are balanced and nutritious so you can perform your best.

# Principle #113

## Never skip breakfast.

Breakfast is the most important meal of the day for everyone, but especially for students. Several studies have proven a direct link between nutritional intake and academic performance. One 2002 study found that schools in which students participated in breakfast programs performed better on tests, attended school more frequently, and participated more effectively in class. Skipping breakfast interferes with learning, memory, and concentration, key skills required for academic excellence. To succeed in school, start your day the right way — with a balanced, nutritious breakfast.

# Principle #114

## Recognize that being overweight will make you miss out.

According to the National Parent Teacher Association (PTA), fit students do best in school because overweight children miss school more often. In fact, overweight students are absent up to 4 times more than fit students! They tend to suffer from medical conditions such as asthma, joint problems, diabetes, high blood pressure, high cholesterol, depression, anxiety, and sleep disorders. These weight-related illnesses not only force students to miss class time, but also prevent students from participating in other school-related activities, such as extracurricular clubs, social groups, and sports. Avoid letting your health sideline you by staying at an average weight.

# Principle #115

## Enroll in an exercise program if you are overweight.

Research shows that being obese hurts both male and female students. One recent study published in *Obesity Research* found that severely overweight girls are more likely than average-weight girls to be held back a grade and to view themselves as stupid or bad at school. Obese boys also tend to consider themselves poor students, and are more likely than average-weight boys to dislike or even hate school. If you are significantly overweight, talk to a counselor, health official, or parent about crafting a diet and weight-loss program that will help you lose weight and get the most out of school.

# Principle #116

## Eat brainpower foods.

While eating nutritious meals is sure to improve your academic performance, certain foods, known as "brainpower foods," should be eaten often, and especially in the days and weeks before big tests. Foods rich in omega-3 fatty acids, vitamin E, magnesium, vitamin C, and vitamins B12 and B6 each support the brain. Some are so effective they are given to patients recovering from brain surgery! The top 10 brainpower foods especially for students include salmon, eggs, beans, spinach, broccoli, cantaloupe, whole grains, berries, tomatoes, citrus fruits, and nuts. See the back of this book for more on how brainpower foods work and why they should be eaten.

# Principle #117

## Avoid foods that malnourish the brain.

Just as some foods give the brain a boost, other foods diminish brain power. Foods high in artery-clogging fats, such as french fries, onion rings, doughnuts, and fried chicken can restrict the flow of blood to the brain. Very sugary foods such as white breads, candy bars, and potatoes can trigger low- and high-blood sugar episodes that make both your body and your mind irritable and sluggish. Of course, alcohol and drugs, such as marijuana, kill brain cells and should be avoided for this and many other reasons. To perform your best in school, replace foods you eat that harm your brain with foods that support it.

# Principle #118

## Cut your soda consumption.

According to the United States Department of Agriculture, as many as 85 percent of students drink a soda every day. In fact, more than 33 percent of all teenagers consume more than 3 servings of soda a day! Soda contributes to weight gain, skin defects, bone density issues, focus and concentration problems, and many other health issues that will affect your ability to perform well in school. Soda contains strong acids such as phosphoric acid, which is so deadly it can dissolve metals (try leaving a penny in a glass of cola overnight!). Be among the first to smarten up by reducing the amount of soda you drink.

# PRINCIPLE #119

## Assess whether your school's lunches are worth eating.

Since child obesity was declared an epidemic in the 21st century, American schools have tried to offer healthier choices to students. According to the Centers for Disease Control and Prevention, as of 2006, only 19 percent of schools continued to serve french fries to students, down from 40 percent in 2000. The percentage of schools that sold cookies or other fattening treats has also dropped. In more than half of all schools, students are now offered water instead of soda in school vending machines, versus 33 percent in 2000. If your school offers healthy snack and lunch choices, feel good about eating there. If not, bring a healthy lunch from home.

# Principle #120

## Participate in physical education classes.

When people think of academic excellence, gym class is not necessarily the first thing that comes to mind. But research indicates that participating in physical education programs can increase a student's test scores. According to a study by the *Journal of School Health*, schools that offer physical education see improved mathematics, reading and writing test scores, and less disruptive behavior, even when participation in gym reduces the amount of time they spend in class. So be sure to get a workout during your school day. As the Roman philosopher Marcus Tullius Cicero observed thousands of years ago, "It is exercise alone that supports the spirits, and keeps the mind in vigor."

# Principle #121

## Get involved in extracurricular sports.

Joining a sports team or otherwise participating in extracurricular athletics is an excellent way to make friends, build a new skill set, and lose weight. In addition, studies show that joining a team can also offer students academic benefits. According to the National Association for Sport and Physical Education and the Council of Physical Education, students who participate in sports report stronger academic performance, increased concentration, better attendance, a more positive attitude toward school, and improved test scores across all major disciplines. If football isn't for you, try tennis, swimming, fencing, the chess club, or other teams your school may offer. Or, investigate private leagues.

# PRINCIPLE #122

## Get a good night's sleep.

Studies show that sleep-deprived students have trouble learning and remembering, and perform poorly on tests. Researchers at Tel Aviv University found that students who were deprived 1 hour of sleep performed 2 grade levels behind their normal ability and age group on tests. Said Ari Sadeh, lead researcher, "A loss of 1 hour of sleep is equivalent to [the loss of] 2 years of cognitive maturation and development." Getting enough sleep is not only critical to performing your best in school, but will improve your skin tone and help you maintain a healthy weight.

# CONTROLLING ANXIETIES

Student anxiety is a problem that has worsened over the last 50 years. San Diego State University Psychology Professor Jean M. Twenge says, "Anxiety that would have put a student in the top 16 percent in the 1950s made a student merely average in the ratings for anxiety in the 1990s." Researchers estimate that about 20 to 30 percent of American students feel anxiety before testing and experience general school-related anxiety in much higher numbers.

Tests are particularly anxiety-causing for students, a fact that fifth-grade teacher Paula Throckmorton learned firsthand. In 2003, she gave a written science test to her class, and every single student failed. However, Throckmorton was convinced the students had failed not because they did not know the material, but because they were too anxious to give the right answers. So she asked them the same questions, but this time in the context of an informal class discussion. Interestingly, almost every student gave the correct answers, answers they could not come up with in test format.

Throckmorton now works to make her classroom environment stress-free, particularly before exams. Before tests, she dresses up in a funny, disarming costume consisting of slippers, a banana nose, and a funny hat. She turns on warm, relaxing classical music, dims the lights, and encourages students to breathe deeply and even meditate before starting the test. During this period her students are able to overcome their anxiety and perform their best on the test. Says Throckmorton, "It makes them dread the test less, and we usually do better on things when we are not afraid."

While all students face anxiety at some point, it is important to remember that stressing over school is more likely to hurt your grade than help it. As the ancient Latin writer Publilius Syrus once quipped, "The bow too tensely strung is easily broken." Use the following simple principles to keep anxiety at bay so you can manage the stress of school in a healthy and productive way.

# Principle #123

## Avoid focusing on your flaws.

Energy wasted dwelling on flaws causes many students to feel unnecessarily anxious. How much time do you waste dwelling on your flaws? Take note how many times a day you think to yourself, "I am too stupid to get into college," or "I am ugly." You will be surprised at how often you single out your most undesirable qualities. Instead of living in a constant state of anxiety about things you cannot change (and that probably aren't true), modify the messages you tell yourself. Start by thinking, "If I can't change this, I am going to embrace it." Instead of fighting your flaws, accept them as part and parcel of who you are.

# Principle #124

## Focus on what you have or can do.

Just as no person is good at everything, there is no person who is not good at something. Think of this truism the next time you are tempted to feel anxious about what you lack or cannot do. Rather than stressing over obstacles, highlight your abilities and talents. Find whatever it is you are good at and throw your energy into that. Use the lessons learned from excelling in one area and apply them to areas in which you are weaker. The writer Maya Angelou once stated, "I believe there is talent in anybody." Find yours and focus on it, especially when you feel anxious.

# Principle #125

## Unplug and take a break.

Anxiety is a widespread problem in our world where everyone is constantly "plugged in." People spend their waking hours tied to email, BlackBerries, cell phones, computers, and other instruments that keep them on the go. Perhaps this is why more than 40 million Americans suffer from an anxiety disorder! If you feel constantly tied down by your electronics, be sure to make time for breaks. Just 20 minutes spent on a quick nap or a relaxing walk away from your gadgets can peel back layers of pent-up anxiety and stress.

# PRINCIPLE #126

## Find a creative outlet to combat anxiety.

—————————— ❉ ——————————

The renowned American author T. S. Eliot once wrote, "Anxiety is the hand maiden of creativity." Eliot knew something about both creativity and anxiety. The next time you feel anxious, try channeling your stress into a creative project. Write a poem or story about the event that has you feeling anxious. If you are a visual person, draw or paint using colors that capture your mood. If you are more crafty, start a project that can take your mind off your problems. Expressing yourself creatively is an excellent way to combat anxiety.

# Principle #127

## Fight anxiety with daydreams.

Focusing on the source of our anxiety can sometimes make it worse. When you start to feel anxious, allow your mind to wander. Go to a place that makes you feel relaxed and happy. Perhaps you sail away on a boat in a beautiful harbor. Maybe you are lying on a beach in Hawaii. No matter where your mind ends up, let it drift and rest there for a little while each day. When you come back, write down what you thought of and how it made you feel. Refer to this daydream book when you're feeling anxious — it will help you remember the sensation of feeling relaxed.

# Principle #128

## Fill your day with positive thoughts.

— ❋ —

Combat anxiety by inserting positive, reassuring thoughts into your daily routine. When you wake, think of the things in life you are good at. Focus on the events and tasks you most look forward to doing that day. Plan to do things you know will give you pleasure and joy, even in small amounts. When settling down at night, review the parts of your day that you did best. If it was a bad day, reassure yourself that you will have opportunities in the coming days to learn from your mistakes and that good things will begin happening to you in the near future.

# PRINCIPLE #129

## Believe in possibilities!

Being optimistic is not only key to being an anxiety-free student, but is key to living a long and healthy life. According to one medical study published in the journal *Archives of General Psychiatry*, optimistic patients have a 55 percent lower risk of death from all causes and 23 percent lower risk of death from heart failure. The ability to look on the bright side, therefore, can translate into not only a stress-free life but a longer one. The next time you start to feel anxious about a situation, focus your efforts on picturing yourself succeeding, and believe in the possibility of making it happen.

# PRINCIPLE #130

## Laugh in the face of anxiety.

Studies show that laughter reduces anxiety, lowers blood pressure, elevates mood, boosts the immune system, improves brain functioning, increases oxygen in the blood, fosters connection with others, and makes you feel good all over. Children in nursery school laugh approximately 300 times a day, while adults laugh, at most, only 17 times per day. How many times did you laugh today? Whatever it was, aim to double it tomorrow. Incorporate a good chuckle into your day to reduce anxiety and promote relaxation. Even though it may feel silly, try to get a good laugh in before a test, presentation, or other stressful academic event.

# PRINCIPLE #131

## Focus on today.

Anxiety is a common problem among students. According to the Anxiety Disorders Association of America (ADAA), school-related anxiety is at a record high. But many of the things that make students anxious occur in the future, such as whether they will pass the final exam or whether they will get into their preferred college. Try keeping your day-to-day anxiety at a minimum by only concerning yourself with things that are happening today. As author Milan Kundera once advised, "The source of anxiety lies in the future. If you can keep the future out of mind, you can forget your worries."

# PRINCIPLE #132

## View setbacks as opportunities.

Setbacks are inevitable, especially in the school environment where you cannot expect to get everything right all the time. Rather than stress over setbacks, think of the great inventor Henry Ford. It was Ford who said, "The setbacks and grieves which we endure help us in our marching onward." The father of the assembly line and the Model T automobile was no stranger to setbacks — he repeatedly hit them while working on his inventions. But Ford always turned adversity into opportunity His reward was crafting many successful inventions that over his lifetime won him 161 U.S. patents. Use Ford to help you remember that viewing setbacks as opportunities is critical for keeping anxiety to a minimum.

# Principle #133

## Ward off anxiety with exercise.

It is true that exercise is an excellent stress-reduction tool, for several reasons. Unused energy turns into tight muscles and tension, which promotes feelings of anxiety and stress. Exercise, however, can help release this built-up tension in the body. Exercise also releases endorphins and other natural mood enhancers, promoting happy, relaxing feelings that naturally combat anxiety. Several studies have shown that regular exercise has a tranquilizer effect. In fact, one study even found exercise more effective at combating anxiety than drugs such as meprobamate, an antidepressant that was popularly known as the original "Happy Pill" in the 1950s. Try to get 30 minutes of exercise several times a week to relieve anxiety.

# PRINCIPLE #134

## Learn deep-breathing techniques that reduce anxiety.

We have been taking breaths since we were born, but few of us know how to breathe properly, even after all this time. Most of us breathe too shallowly to harness the relaxing benefits of breathing. Breathing properly requires you to inhale deeply using your diaphragm, not your chest. This moves air through your whole respiratory system, not just your upper lungs. Inhale for a count of 5. Hold your breath briefly, then slowly exhale through your mouth for another count of 5. Relax every part of your body as you exhale. Repeat several times. Carve out 5 minutes from every day to focus on concentrated breathing to minimize episodes of anxiety.

# PRINCIPLE #135

## Practice yoga to unwind.

The health benefits of yoga are far-reaching and varied. In addition to improving flexibility and muscle tone, the daily practice of yoga can drastically minimize a person's tendency to feel anxious. Regular yoga practice forces you to breathe deeply, which increases the blood flow and oxygen to your limbs and organs. These physical benefits lead to a sense of calm and relaxation. Many yoga poses are easy to learn and can be done in your bedroom or other small space. Learn a few poses you can call on when anxiety starts to creep up.

# Principle #136

## Realize that anxiety interferes with your studies.

Rose Kennedy, mother of former President John F. Kennedy and Senator Robert Kennedy, once said, "Neither comprehension nor learning can take place in an atmosphere of anxiety." Having raised 2 extremely successful men, she was intimately familiar with anxiety's effects on a person's ability to concentrate in school. Ironically, the best students are anxious about school-related matters but fail to realize it is their very anxiety that threatens them academically. It is normal and even useful to feel alert, even nervous, before big academic events. But avoid feeling anxious about them, as you are sure to do yourself more harm than good.

# GETTING SUPPORT

If school were something that could be accomplished on one's own, students could simply sit in a room by themselves with books and a computer until they passed their tests and earned their diplomas. But getting an education is an interactive endeavor and, at times, involves getting in touch with those who can support you academically. Teachers, principals, counselors, librarians, parents, tutors, specialists, and peers are just a few of the people who should play a part in your academic support network.

Students need support at different times in their academic careers. Some students require extra help just before a big quiz or test; others need help practicing their writing, reading, and research skills all semester long. Students need help if they don't know how to go about gathering information, if they have little or no interaction with their teachers due to large class size, or if they have trouble disciplining themselves to get their work done on time. Still, other students require support if they have been diagnosed with a learning disability, don't have access to high-end learning tools such as computers or personal copies of books, or if they learn drastically differently from other students in their class.

For each of these problems, there is a person in your extended academic support network who can help you. The key is to identify these people and seek out their services before it is too late to turn your grades around. To figure out who you can turn to for help, examine in which area you need it most. Then, discuss with your parents or teachers the most appropriate person to get you that help.

Relying on the support of others is nothing to be embarrassed about — all students need help now and then. Not as many students, however, are smart enough to ask for it. The following simple principles will give you ideas for places and people to ask for help. Do not hesitate to contact them when you are struggling academically or socially.

# PRINCIPLE #137

## Avoid getting lost in the crowd.

Overcrowded schools and increased classroom size have made it easy to get lost in the crowd. According to the National Center for Education Statistics, the average student-teacher ratio in American high schools is 16:1, but most classes tend to be larger due to the fact that special teachers who work with small groups — such as speech therapists — are factored into the ratio. In reality, classes often have 30, even 40 students crowded in a room together. Make every effort to introduce yourself to teachers and administrators so they can get to know you. Being more than just a face in a crowd will help you avoid getting lost in it.

# Principle #138

## Take advantage of office hours.

All college professors, and most high school teachers, hold office hours. These are a few hours each week devoted to answering students' questions and giving individualized help. Taking advantage of office hours is an excellent way to get academic support. Use these hours to clarify points made in a lecture, help with your homework, to double-check notes copied from the board, or to find out what material is going to be covered on a test. If for some reason you can't make a teacher's office hours, ask that they schedule you in at another time. You will find that most teachers are so supportive of a student's interest in getting help that they will work around your schedule.

# PRINCIPLE #139

## Get your teacher's attention during class.

According to a study by Indiana University, 31 percent of all high school students are bored in class because they lack interaction with their teacher. Said Ethan Yazzie-Mintz, the study's director, "Students [are] sitting there and not interacting with a teacher on a daily basis and maybe never. They're not having those interactions, which we know are critical for student engagement with learning... ." Teacher-student interaction is increasingly difficult due to expanding class size, but is important for doing well in school. Get your teacher's attention by participating in class, volunteering for assignments or extra credit, or otherwise positively contributing to the classroom.

# Principle #140

## Hire a tutor.

A tutor is a great source from which to get academic support that busy parents and teachers are unable to provide. A tutor can help you drill problems, go in depth with material, and tailor explanations of difficult subjects to your learning style. Sometimes, a tutor is most valuable for simply holding a student accountable for homework and readings. As the English philosopher John Locke once said, "It is easier for a tutor to command than to teach." Look into hiring a tutor to support you academically. Students with special needs, such as economically disadvantaged or learning-disabled students, can be eligible to receive free tutoring from their school.

# PRINCIPLE #141

## Participate in a peer-advisory program.

Multiple studies have shown that in the right environment, peers make excellent teachers. With this in mind, many schools have found success in peer-advisory programs. In these programs, a student who excels in a particular subject mentors a student who needs help. The peer advisors tend to be older and more academically advanced than the students they mentor. Investigate whether your school offers a peer advisory program. If your school does not offer one, ask officials if one can be started, and volunteer to pilot it. Ask your teachers to recommend students who would make good advisors, and seek them out on your own. Or, if you are academically gifted, offer to tutor other students yourself.

# Principle #142

## Let your parents help you — they were students once, too.

Although it may seem as if your parents are ancient, they were once students just like you. They probably studied similar subjects and have, as adults, learned even more about them. Enlist your family's help in giving you academic support. They can help you complete homework; explain difficult concepts to you; or put information in historical, political, or geographical context. At the very least, your parents can help proofread your papers. Before turning anything in, ask your mother, father, or older sibling to proofread what you've written. Give them a hard copy so they can mark it up and make comments in the margins.

# PRINCIPLE #143

## Find a helping hand at the library.

Libraries are often-overlooked resources in the digital era. Many students skip the library and search for information online from their home computer. But the Internet is only a useful tool if you know how to use it, and students usually collect information that is not authoritative. Computers in the library, however, use databases that are prescreened for reputable material. Furthermore, librarians are excellent stewards of information. They will be able to help you find information you need. As millionaire Malcolm Forbes once said, "The richest person in the world — in fact all the riches in the world — couldn't provide you with anything like the endless, incredible loot available at your local library."

# Principle #144

## Recognize that support can only help so much.

All the support in the world will not help a student who is unwilling to take the reins on their education. It is important to recognize that the people and resources that can help you advance academically are only able to help you in proportion to the amount you help yourself. In other words, you must be willing to do the bulk of your work. Your academic support network is not meant to be used to get you out of jams or save you from your own laziness. People can help, but ultimately, you will have to stay motivated and complete your work yourself.

# DEALING WITH PEER PRESSURE

Experiencing peer pressure is an inevitable part of being human. At all ages, we interact with peers who influence our ideas, values, and decisions. As a person gets older and becomes more comfortable with themselves, however, they care less how they are viewed, and feel more confident that people will like them even if they go against the grain. But young adults are particularly vulnerable to peer pressure because they are still struggling to figure who they are and what they value. They do not have confidence that they will be liked if they act differently from their peers. Walt Mueller, author of *Understanding Today's Youth Culture*, says, "The ugly reality is that peer pressure reaches its greatest intensity at just the age when kids tend to be most insensitive and cruel" — and when they have the fewest number of defenses against it.

There are many forms of peer pressure that contemporary students must contend with. Some forms of peer pressure involve ganging up on an outcast, feeling pressured to talk about your friends behind their backs, or feeling forced to prove yourself by doing something you wouldn't ordinarily do. Other forms can lead students down destructive, even illegal, paths. Even the best students have been known to be peer pressured into cheating, lying, cutting class, smoking, stealing, and trying dangerous drugs.

The two activities teens are most often peer pressured into are having sex and drinking. According to a study published in *Psychology Today*, many teens, especially boys, feel pressure to have sex before they are ready. Despite the fact that 63 percent of teens think waiting to have sex is a good idea, few of them actually do because of peer pressure to lose their virginities as soon as possible. The pressure to drink also comes down heavy on the nation's students. According to the U.S. Surgeon General's office, 10.6 million teens are drinkers, and nearly 80 percent of high school students interviewed said they drank because of pressure from their friends.

Interestingly, peer pressure is often more subtle than a challenge issued directly from one student to another. At times, peer pressure exists simply in the form of an idea. An example is smoking. Even if none of their friends has directly challenged them to smoke, many students feel peer pressured to smoke because of the concept that smoking is cool and rebellious. A 2005 study published in the *Journal of Studies on Alcohol*, provides an example. After surveying students on 130 college campuses, researchers found that about 75 percent of students overestimated the amount of heavy drinking going on around them. In reality, the number of students who abused alcohol was quite low, but the mere notion that many of their peers were drinking led some students to drink excessively.

For such a small word, "no" can be the most difficult for some students to say when faced with peer pressure. "No" gets easier to say when you have a strong sense of who you are, what you value, and the self-confidence to stand your ground in the face of a challenge. The following simple principles will help you gain the self-confidence you need to resist peer pressure, and also give you tips, tricks, and ideas for reducing its power in your life.

# Principle #145

## Silence your inner critic.

Students who succumb to peer pressure tend to have low self-esteem. Thinking they are less than worthy leads them to be pressured into smoking, drinking, stealing, lying, cheating, or other bad behaviors, in an attempt to show others how cool they are. Therefore, the first step to becoming immune to peer pressure is to silence the critic within yourself. As an African proverb states, "When there is no enemy within, the enemies outside cannot hurt you." The truly cool don't let anyone talk them into doing something they don't want to do, because they have silenced the voice of self-doubt within. Be proud of every time you say "no" to peer pressure.

# Principle #146

## Be yourself, not what other people expect you to be.

All of us are members of some race, gender, ethnicity, religion, or social group. Such membership offers solidarity and a sense of identity, but it can also come with an expectation to be like everyone else in that group. The pressure to fit in with a group is at the heart of peer pressure. Avoid this pressure by always maintaining your individuality. If the tenet, behavior, or attitude of a group does not match up with who you truly are, reject that portion of it. Demanding that others treat you as an individual (and treating others similarly) will reduce the power of peer pressure.

# Principle #147

## Think about yourself positively.

The best way to deal with peer pressure is to have high self-esteem, and the best way to cultivate self-esteem is to use the most powerful tool you have — your thoughts. Every negative or nasty thing you tell yourself throughout the day ("I'm stupid," "I'm ugly," "My butt is too big," "I am such a loser") erodes your self-esteem. These thoughts should be replaced with positive messages you tell yourself, such as, "I look good today," or "I'm smarter than I give myself credit for." Positive self-talk leads to a positive self-image, which will reduce the effect power peer pressure is able to have on you.

# Principle #148

## Choose your friends wisely.

Studies have repeatedly shown that friends are the biggest factor in whether a student will be vulnerable to peer pressure. Therefore, it is important to make friends with people who respect and share your values. When you have friends who like you for who you are, there is no need to prove yourself or feel subject to peer pressure. Make friends with people who will not test or tempt you to do stupid things just to fit in. As philosopher Elbert Hubbard said, "A friend is one who knows you and loves you just the same." Surround yourself with friends who accept you as you are, and love you for it.

# Principle #149

## Make at least one friend who will say "no" with you.

The hardest part about dealing with peer pressure is being the only one with the guts to say "no" to destructive behavior. Therefore, try and have at least one friend you can count on to say "no" with you. Having a partner makes it easier to resist the power of peer pressure, and will give the two of you something to bond over. Find one friend who also knows that smoking is terrible for your health, or who also agrees that drinking and driving is not cool. Together you can feel good about not succumbing to peer pressure — and don't be surprised when others follow your lead.

# Principle #150

## Be proud of your flaws.

Each of us has something we cannot change. But many students allow their flaws to make them vulnerable to peer pressure. For example, the girl who is slightly overweight may be peer pressured into smoking to curb her appetite. The boy who is short may be peer pressured into stealing to come off like a big man. Instead of letting a flaw make you vulnerable to peer pressure, present it as something that makes you unique. The pride and self-confidence that comes from owning your shortcomings will help you avoid being peer pressured into doing something to compensate for those flaws.

# PRINCIPLE #151

## Develop your own voice, and listen to it.

———————— ✳ ————————

The average American child is exposed to more than 40,000 commercial messages each year. These messages are delivered through television, print, radio, and Internet programming, and their whole point is to make you believe that something is missing from your life. If you believe you lack something, you will buy products to fill that need. But believing you lack something primes you to be vulnerable to peer pressure. In fact, advertising is, in itself, a form of peer pressure! Learning to develop your own voice will reduce your vulnerability to messages that infer you are not good enough. This will help you stand up to peer pressure in its multiple forms.

# PRINCIPLE #152

## Avoid comparing yourself to others.

— ❊ —

While it is tempting to look around you for validation, your best measuring stick is, in fact, yourself. Focus on recognizing your own strengths and weaknesses without comparing yourself to others. The truth of the matter is that someone, somewhere can and will score higher, run faster, or look better than you. If you fixate on what other people have, you will be more susceptible to peer pressure, which will reduce your ability to accomplish something truly incredible in your own right. Avoid getting caught up in doing things just to outdo someone else. Instead, feel satisfied knowing you are doing your best and doing a great job at that.

# PRINCIPLE #153

## Let go of the perfectionist complex.

While some students feel peer pressured to behave dangerously, others feel pressure to be perfect. Indeed, some schools are so competitive that students drive themselves crazy and even make themselves sick trying to keep up. If this describes your school, realize that while it is wonderful to set high standards, you must avoid becoming obsessed with being perfect. As the actor George Fisher once put it, "When you aim for perfection, you discover it's a moving target." Indeed, chasing perfection is a never-ending battle, because it is a state that cannot be attained. Instead, aim to try your hardest, do your best, and know when to be satisfied with your performance.

# Principle #154

## Learn to love the way you look.

❈

According to Planet Project, a global Internet polling company that polled 380,000 people in more than 225 countries, about 65 percent of the world's population is unhappy with the way they look. Teenagers are especially self-loathing — they are the group mostly commonly affected by eating disorders and other body-harming disorders such as cutting and self-mutilation. But every second you spend hating your body is truly wasted time. Start realizing today that your body is perfect as it ought to be, and it is better for you to celebrate it than resent it. Encourage your friends to do the same, and you will surround yourself with peers that encourage your success and self-esteem, not detract from it.

# Principle #155

## Don't give peer pressure permission to make you feel inferior.

— ❋ —

Most students give in to peer pressure because they don't want to be seen as uncool or socially inferior to others. However, only you have the power to allow yourself to feel uncool. As the great American comedian W.C. Fields once said, "It ain't what they call you, it's what you answer to." With this in mind, aim to elevate yourself above the petty insults, challenges, and criticisms of others. Know that you are better than someone who has so little self-regard that he will put other people down in hopes of proving he is cool.

# Principle #156

## Don't fall for peer pressure.

———————————— ✳ ————————————

Resisting peer pressure is important because it helps you develop as an individual, which prevents you from becoming a victim of group-thinking. The next time peer pressure tempts you to go along with those doing something wrong, stand up for yourself and what's right. If you don't and you are caught, you will likely be punished and your parents will be disappointed in you for failing to stand your ground in the face of peer pressure. As author Richard Bach has astutely written, "If it's never our fault, we can't take responsibility for it. If we can't take responsibility for it, we'll always be its victim."

# Principle #157

## Trust your instincts.

When faced with peer pressure, rely on your instincts — they have been scientifically proven to best guide you. A 2006 study published in the journal *Science* found that people who face complex decisions choose better when they follow their guts. Indeed, former CEO of Hewlett-Packard, Carly Fiorina, has said, "You have to master not only the art of listening to your head, you must also master listening to your heart and listening to your gut." Clearly, Fiorina is no stranger to listening to her gut to guide her toward right decisions and away from wrong ones. When a peer tries to get you to do something that you feel in your gut is wrong, it probably is.

# PRINCIPLE #158

## Resist the urge to run your decisions past your friends.

Asking friends their opinion can be a good way to make all kinds of decisions, such as how short to cut your hair or where to apply to college. But many students listen to others so often that they become unable to make a decision without the input of others. By listening to too many voices, you are likely to end up discounting your own. So refrain from involving too many people in your decision-making process. As motivational speaker Jim Rohn has advised, "If you don't design your own life plan, chances are you'll fall into someone else's plan. And guess what they have planned for you? Not much."

# Principle #159

## Talk to someone trustworthy.

If you find it difficult to combat peer pressure on your own, reach out to someone trustworthy for help. This could be a parent, teacher, older sibling, school counselor, coach, or other authority figure that you trust or respect. Ask them to help you deal with whatever peer pressure you are facing. Above all, don't wait to ask for help. Combating peer pressure is a skill you will need throughout life, as peer pressure can affect adults for decades. As comedian Dennis Wolfberg has joked, "There's one advantage to being 102. There's no peer pressure." Don't wait until then to get help dealing with peer pressure — ask someone you trust today.

# Creating A Positive
# Social Environment

As much as some adults would like to pretend that school is all about classes, tests, and learning, much of a student's school experience is dependant upon his or her social experience. Indeed, a student's social environment in school is in many ways as important as the educational one, especially because the happier and more socially adjusted a student is, the more he or she is bound to succeed at school. If a student likes going to school and feels comfortable there, he or she is more likely to excel in all school-related areas.

Making, having, and keeping friends, therefore, is as important to excelling in school as studying, taking notes, and doing homework. Education is not the only area of life that is made better by the presence of friends. In 2005, a ground-breaking research study published in the *Journal of Epidemiology and Community Health* found that having a network of good friends can extend a person's life span. After studying thousands of people for more than a decade, researchers found that close contact with relatives has surprisingly little impact on how long a person lives. However, a close network of good friends and confidantes significantly improved a person's chances of living longer.

One of the life-giving benefits of friendship is that friends often provide a person with something that family members may not: a supportive, nonjudgmental, accepting environment that helps a person cope with frustration, sadness, and challenge. Friends nurture talents and interests in each other that family sometimes fail to appreciate; they also tend to "get" each other in ways that family often do not. These emotional support networks are important because they enable a person to succeed in other areas of life, such as school.

If you want to excel at school, you will have to make it a place you enjoy going every day. That will entail engaging the social elements of school, such as having friends, attending events, and joining teams and clubs. The following simple principles will help you make friends and take part in activities that will make your school experience more positive, interesting, and even fun!

# PRINCIPLE #160

## Don't hide behind technology.

Technological marvels such as email and cell phones allow us to be in touch with 10 times the number of people that could be communicated with in simpler times of landlines and letters. Yet these advances in technology have resulted in a severe decline in interpersonal relationships. This is because interactions that take place via a device are limited in depth and emotion. To make true friends, avoid hiding behind technology. Call instead of text messaging; visit instead of emailing. Aim for establishing a real, personal link with everyone you are "friends" with on MySpace or Facebook. This is the only way to make meaningful friends who will stick by you through the years.

# PRINCIPLE #161

## Seek meaningful
## interactions with friends.

Our fast-paced society makes it hard to find time for meaningful interactions with people. It is easy to chat between classes or leave a voicemail and then feel like you have made the effort to connect. These superficial communications are no substitute for an in-depth getting-to-know-you session. In order to develop real friendships, you must put time and energy into nurturing them. So meet your friend for coffee, a concert, or a game. Send him or her a handwritten birthday card in the mail. Going these extra lengths will endear you to the people you care about most.

# PRINCIPLE #162

## Participate in school-sponsored activities.

It is likely your school has a multitude of social activities you can take part in. Most schools host pep rallies, socials, dances, performances, sports games, and other events. Get in the habit of attending at least 1 school-sponsored social event a month. At these events, you will meet others with similar interests. You will also form a friendship over a particular event or memory, which can be quite bonding. Participate in as many events as you can, if not for the simple reason that it will make your school life more fun. As the French author Antoine de Saint-Exupery wrote, "What am I if I am not a participant? In order to be, I must participate."

# Principle #163

## Turn strangers into friends.

Actress Shirley Maclaine once remarked, "Fear makes strangers of people who would be friends." Indeed, don't let a fear of being rejected prevent you from making new friends! If you are lonely for new friends, strike up conversation with someone you meet at a party, through a club, or on a sports team. Invite them to do something after school. It may feel awkward to be so forward, but work through that. Making friends definitely involves putting yourself out there — but once you do, you are sure to be surrounded by many new friends.

# PRINCIPLE #164

## Create two-sided conversations.

A common conversational pitfall made by many students is to have one-sided conversations that focus solely on them. Many students, when asked where they live or if they play a sport or instrument, provide answers without asking the same of the person with whom they are speaking. When you fail to reciprocate questions, you indicate a lack of interest in other people. Always make sure you get an answer to the same questions that were asked of you. A simple, "What about you?" or "How was your weekend?" creates a dialogue that shows you care and can be the start of a valuable friendship.

# PRINCIPLE #165

## Participate in extracurricular activities.

A survey of more than 50,000 Minnesota high school students, published in the March 2003 issue of the *Journal of School Health,* found that those who participated in extracurricular activities had higher levels of social, emotional, and physically healthy behavior than students who did not. Seek out the extracurricular activities offered at your school. There are bound to be clubs, teams, or charitable organizations that will appeal to some aspect of your personality. Participating in extracurricular activities will make you feel better about yourself and your school, help you make friends, and will be a high point on the applications you send to colleges.

# PRINCIPLE #166

## Start a club to meet people with similar interests.

Everyone has something they care about. If your school doesn't provide a club for your particular interest or cause, start one! Usually all you need to start a club is a mission statement and the support of a teacher. Your club could be charity-related, and meetings could focus on ways to get involved in the community. Or, your club could be hobby-related, and tie together people with a common interest in a certain type of music, art, computers, or other skill. Starting a new club is likely to draw other students with the same interests out of the woodwork. Additionally, being the creator of a school organization will look extremely impressive on a college application.

# Principle #167

## Include the new kid.

It is never easy being new to a school. Be sensitive to this difficulty the next time someone new comes to your school. Welcome this person. Don't leave it up to him or her to figure out what you are talking about — have the courtesy to catch him or her up in conversation. Let the new kid in on an inside joke. Ask what he or she thinks about the question at hand. Giving the new person room to make a positive first impression establishes a friendly tone and gives a much-needed confidence boost to those who might otherwise be shy. Including a new student will also establish you as a social leader that others will look up to.

# Principle #168

## Dress appropriately to show you're serious about learning.

Though judging someone by their appearance might seem superficial, people do it every day. How you dress reflects the pride you take in yourself. A sloppy appearance conveys that you don't care or aren't serious about learning. Instead, come to school dressed neatly and appropriately. This shows respect for yourself, your teachers, and your fellow classmates. While it is OK to express your personality through what you wear, always be respectful of the school environment. This means staying away from things like short skirts and dirty or ripped clothes. If you dress neatly and appropriately, people will know you are serious about excelling at school.

# PRINCIPLE #169

## Be there for your friends.

— ❋ —

Maintaining friendships can sometimes take a lot of work!
You must be willing to invest your time in phone calls,
parties, games, outings, and one-on-one time. To make good
friends and have them at your disposal, you must be available
for them when they need it. Realize that it takes a lot of work
to have a close-knit circle and to make time, at any hour, to
be a good friend. Be intuitive to others' needs; for instance,
recognize if a friend has a big test coming up and offer to
help him study. Follow up afterward by asking him how the
test went. As the poet Robert Brault once quipped, "I value
the friend who for me finds time on his calendar, but I cherish
the friend who for me does not consult his calendar."

# Principle #170

## Avoid cliques.

At most schools, cliques are as much a reality as classes, tests, and assemblies. Social cliques are inherently a part of school because most young adults lack the confidence to strike out on their own. Being surrounded by a group of friends that thinks, talks, and looks exactly like them makes them feel more comfortable, even powerful. But you will probably have a more positive school experience if you avoid becoming part of one clique. Instead, think of your group of friends as a collection — each one should be slightly different from each other, and slightly different from you. This is a winning recipe for long-lasting friendships that go beyond superficial connections.

# PRINCIPLE #171

## Be best friends with yourself.

---- ✳ ----

The relationship you have with yourself is the foundation for the friendships you make with others. If you seek joy only in others, you will always be looking for happiness in the wrong place. Furthermore, if you dislike yourself, potential friends will have no reason to like you. Indeed, the love and respect you have for yourself is directly proportional to the love and respect your friends are able to feel for you. Most people can tell when a person likes or dislikes themself, and treats them accordingly. As actress Lucille Ball once said, "Love yourself first and everything else falls into line."

# SETTING EDUCATIONAL GOALS

Author Arnold H. Glasow once said, "Success isn't a result of spontaneous combustion. You must set yourself on fire." Indeed, succeeding in school and becoming someone you are proud of does not happen overnight, or accidentally. Rather, it is the result of hard work, careful planning, and articulating and reaching goals. Setting educational goals is both a long- and short-term process that students should start practicing in high school.

When setting goals, it is important not to worry so much about picking a career. While previous generations were encouraged to stick with one profession, workers of the 21st century are increasingly fluid and mobile. In fact, most modern professionals change careers 3 or 4 times over the course of their working life. They go to back to school in their 30s, even 40s, and never worry that it is "too late" to begin pursuing new goals. Indeed, it is too early for you to organize your goals around a specific career. Instead, articulate goals based on skill sets or personal interests that could be applied to several fields, such as writing, building computers, or designing objects.

Another key factor of successful goal-setting is setting the bar where you can reach it. The way to craft sensible, realistic goals is to break larger goals into smaller ones you can tackle in the immediate future. If your ultimate educational goal is to become proficient in French, put it at the top of your list. Note the steps required to make this goal a reality — taking French classes in school; traveling to places where French is spoken; sparking a pen-pal relationship with a French-speaking student; getting a summer internship that requires you to use French; becoming a French tutor, and so on. Check off when you accomplish tasks that feed your larger goal. Chipping away at the larger goal by tackling its more manageable aspects will put you in a position to make your top goal a reality.

The following principles will help you set and achieve both long- and short-term educational goals. Begin implementing them in your everyday life so you can get the most out of school and life.

# PRINCIPLE #172

## Write an educational mission statement.

Being a successful student means having a clear idea of what you hope to accomplish in school and beyond. Writing a mission statement will help you pinpoint where to focus your efforts. Your mission statement should clearly state the things about school and learning that are most important to you. It should reflect goals based on these values. Your mission statement should be motivational, easy to understand, and action-oriented. Someone who reads it should have a clear idea of what kind of student you are, what you like to study, what you hope to get out of school, and what career you might end up in. An example of a mission statement is, "I will excel in the sciences and get good enough grades that I can apply to a college known for its engineering program."

# Principle #173

## Be realistic when you set your goals.

— ❈ —

Business tycoon Warren Buffett once said, "I don't look to jump over 7-foot bars; I look around for 1-foot bars that I can step over." Buffett was commenting on the importance of being realistic when you set your goals. Instead of resolving to get straight A's this semester, start by trying to get A's in 1 or 2 classes. Next semester, challenge yourself to get a few more A's. Realistic goals are those you are willing and able to reach. Setting the bar out of reach will only frustrate you and make you consider giving up. Studies consistently show that setting goals and working toward achieving them is one of the most significant ways to see results, no matter what you are attempting.

# PRINCIPLE #174

## Articulate your short-term educational goals.

To jump-start your feeling of accomplishment, keep a list of short-term goals. These can be things you can accomplish on a daily or weekly basis. Some can be assignments that need to be completed, or a certain number of chapters you'd like to read before the next class. Others can be activities you've been meaning to do but haven't gotten around to in a while, such as revisiting old notes, cleaning out your desk, or making an appointment with a college counselor. Cross items off your list as you do them. This will give you an immediate sense of accomplishment and will keep you motivated to tackle your larger goals.

# Principle #175

## Articulate your long-term educational goals.

Consider your long-term goals — those that take extensive planning and many steps to achieve. Do you want to challenge yourself to get into a top-tier college? Do you want to get an advanced degree, such as a master's or Ph.D? Do you know what career you'd like to train for? Do you want to study in another country? Write down your long-term goals, put them in a highly visible place, and look at them often. Viewing these milestones will remind you of what you want to accomplish and what it will take to get there. As educator Lawrence J. Peter once said, "If you don't know where you are going, you will probably end up somewhere else. "

# PRINCIPLE #176

## Allow yourself to hope and dream.

If setting educational goals sounds formal and makes you panic, don't stress. Setting goals is nothing more than tapping into your hopes, dreams, and wild ideas. Indeed, fantasies and dreams and are often the pillars on which we can base attainable goals. As author Diana Scharf Hunt once put it, "Goals are dreams with deadlines." Let your mind wander and see where it leads you. Write down when you feel particularly inspired by an idea for the future. Avoid telling yourself it is stupid, you can't achieve it, or you will never be able to make money in such a way. Just concentrate on pinpointing academic areas that will help you attain your goals.

# Principle #177

## Research how others have achieved their goals.

Sitting down with your list of goals can be daunting. Your first thought will likely be, "Where do I begin?" Once you articulate your goals, figure out what steps you must take to achieve them by researching the path of people who have already accomplished similar goals. If your goal is to graduate high school with honors, find out what other honors students have done to make it happen. If your goal is to become a veterinarian, research how many years of school and what kinds of prerequisites are required to apply to vet school. Or, take it a step further and identify someone in your school or city that has been successful in your area of interest, and use him or her as a mentor.

# PRINCIPLE #178

## Share goals with others.

Whether it is a public declaration, collaboration, or friendly competition, it is important to involve others in the process of setting and achieving your educational goals. By letting others know you have set a goal for yourself, they keep you accountable to it. For instance, once you have told friends and relatives that you will be taking an honors history class you will be less likely to go back on your word, for fear of having to make excuses or letting down the people close to you. Never do things just for the sake of having something to share with others, but do use the people in your life as motivation for following through on the goals you told them you would.

# PRINCIPLE #179

## Avoid taking shortcuts to achieve your goals.

Hard, honest work makes reaching a goal a satisfying, rewarding, and enriching experience. Taking shortcuts to your goals, however, fails to achieve the same results. If accomplishing a goal means you must employ shortcuts such as cheating, lying, stealing, copying, or fraud, you should stop your efforts right now. Reaching your goal through nefarious means never justifies the end result, and nullifies the point of having a goal in the first place. As opera singer Beverly Sills once observed, "There are no shortcuts to any place worth going."

# Principle #180

## Be willing to work diligently.

Stephen King once wrote, "Talent is cheaper than table salt. What separates the talented individual from the successful one is a lot of hard work." King is no stranger to hard work — becoming a renowned author takes not only talent, but hard work, discipline, patience, and perseverance. Through hard work, King turned his talent into 50 best-selling books, and is one of the most successful horror and fantasy writers in America. Like King, you will have to work diligently to turn your talent into achievable goals. Have no illusions that achieving your goals will be easy or quick, but the rewards and satisfaction you will receive will be worth the work and the wait.

# Principle #181

## Be curious about ... everything!

As you experiment with the process of setting educational goals, it is important to avoid shutting doors on subjects, opportunities, or ideas you think are not right for you. You cannot achieve worthwhile goals if you shut yourself off to new opportunities. Trying new things will help you learn what you like and don't like. Furthermore, cultivating curiosity will help you become a lifelong learner, which will help you in any pursuit. As educator Clay P. Bedford has said, "You can teach a student a lesson for a day; but if you can teach him to learn by creating curiosity, he will continue the learning process as long as he lives."

# PRINCIPLE #182

## Don't let past failures prevent you from starting over.

The wonderful thing about learning is you have countless opportunities to grow. Unfortunately, many students allow a poor track record to keep them down. They feel like they will never be able to recover from a failed test, poor grade, or mediocre attendance record, and so they continue the undesirable behavior. Never let yesterday's failures prevent you from starting anew and reaching your goals. As author Carl Bard once put it, "Though no one can go back and make a brand-new start, anyone can start from now and make a brand-new ending." Modify destructive behaviors today and you will quickly find yourself back on the path to success.

# Principle #183

## Be a lifelong learner
## to achieve your dreams.

It will take perseverance, patience, and ingenuity, but if you want it bad enough, you can make your dreams come true. Above all, never allow petty excuses like "I am not smart enough," or "I don't have enough time," to derail you from reaching your goals. Should these thoughts start to creep in, recall what H. Jackson Brown Jr., editor of *Life's Little Instruction Book*, has said about reaching one's goals: "Don't say you don't have enough time. You have exactly the same number of hours per day that were given to Helen Keller, Pasteur, Michaelangelo, Mother Teresea, Leonardo da Vinci, Thomas Jefferson, and Albert Einstein."

# Applying to Colleges and Universities

Going to college is the culmination of your studies and the main reason why you have worked so hard throughout high school. In the 21st century, a college education is a must for succeeding in life. According to a 2007 College Board Study, adults who received a bachelor's degree earn more than 60 percent more than those with only a high school diploma. Over a lifetime, the gap in earning potential can amount to more than $800,000!

Furthermore, those with only a high school diploma are 3 times more likely than those with a bachelor's degree to be unemployed. Those with bachelor's degrees are also more likely to be more consistently employed, work in better conditions, receive better benefits, travel more, and have more hobbies than those who capped their education at high school. Surveys by the Public Health Service have even found that those who attended college are better educated about healthy habits and lifestyle, and thus tend to live longer than those who are not college educated.

Going to college offers many social benefits as well. In the 21st century, college is viewed as a rite of passage for young adults. It is in college where people discover the interests and skills that will usher them into adulthood and make friends that will last a lifetime. It is where students learn to care about the world around them, think critically about pressing issues of the day, and develop their identity apart from their family. Most important, it is a special and rare part of life in which the majority of time will be devoted to learning, instead of making an income and paying bills.

Finally, college offers students the chance to study what they truly enjoy. While high school turns many students off to learning because it forces them to take a core curriculum filled with subjects they may not enjoy, college offers students the freedom to specialize in the arts, sciences, humanities, or vocational pursuits. Together, these qualities make the college experience one of the most fun, interesting, and unique periods of life.

But before you reap any of these benefits, you have to be accepted. The process of applying to college has become intensely competitive and hugely expensive. According to the Education Resource Information Center, college preparation is a $2 billion-a-year industry, with some parents spending more than $5,000 to get their children college-ready.

You don't need to spend thousands of dollars to ready yourself for college, however. In fact, the biggest boost you can give your application is completely free: your time. Indeed, those who start planning and preparing for college early are most likely to have high acceptance rates to schools of their choice.

How to make the most of the time before you apply to college is just one of the topics covered in the following simple principles. The following tips, tricks, and ideas will help you understand what is required of a college applicant so you can improve your candidacy to the school of your dreams.

# Principle #184

## Realize that the college-application process begins freshman year.

Your application to college reflects your academics and activities throughout high school, so think ahead. Too often, seniors find themselves barred from a particular college because of poor grades from early semesters. It is extremely important to start *and* finish strong. Additionally, colleges will note if you have made steady progress over the years in a subject that is more difficult for you. Also, make sure you know the class requirements for the colleges you are applying to well in advance. Will you need 2 years of a foreign language? Will it be advantageous to take calculus? Keep on top of your grades and class load from the start.

# PRINCIPLE #185

## Get ahead by taking honors classes.

Signing up for honors or AP classes can provide tremendous benefits when applying to college. When colleges see honors courses on your transcript, they will value the fact that you challenged yourself in high school. Taking honors classes shows that you enjoy learning and appreciate a challenge. Even more important perhaps is that AP classes can get you college credit; you can test out of lower-level college courses and, oftentimes, even graduate from college early. While you might be hesitant to take an advanced class because it may be more difficult, remember that honors courses will better prepare you for the workload and expectations you will find in college.

# PRINCIPLE #186

## Use your college counselor or hire an expert.

Make an appointment to meet with the college counselor at your school. It is the job of college counselors to be intimately familiar with colleges around the country, even around the world, and to help you hone in on a handful that are right for you. Your counselor can advise you as to which classes to take in high school, make recommendations about extracurricular activities to highlight on your application, and keep you informed about test-registration and application deadlines. If your school's college counselor is inadequate or your school does not have one, consider hiring an expert to help guide you through the application process.

# Principle #187

## Keep track of your extracurricular activities.

Colleges desire students who are interesting, well-rounded, talented, charitable, and natural leaders. For this reason, your extracurricular activities should be prominently featured on your college application. Avoid losing track of what you've done by starting a folder for all your extracurricular activities and achievements. In this folder, place any diplomas, awards, and certificates you have received. Keep a running list of athletic trophies, varsity letters, or musical awards you have won. Also keep track of any school or community organizations you join, volunteer work you do, offices you hold, jobs you have, and special projects you participate in.

# Principle #188

## Take the PSAT.

While 85 percent of all high school seniors take the SATs, far fewer take the PSAT, or practice SAT. The PSAT is usually offered to 10th- and 11th-graders seeking practice for the SAT test. There are several reasons to take the PSAT. The PSAT mimics the testing content and conditions of the real SAT, giving you a chance to prepare for that test. Furthermore, your score will not be sent to colleges, so if you do poorly it cannot hurt you. Finally, some colleges seeking junior achievers offer merit scholarships based on PSAT scores. For all these reasons, make sure you take the PSAT in either your sophomore or junior year.

# PRINCIPLE #189

## Avoid padding your college application.

❋

In a mad rush to impress college-entrance committees, some students join every organization under the sun to make themselves appear involved and diverse. But college acceptance committees don't appreciate superficial extracurricular involvement. They are looking for students to make meaningful, ongoing commitments to organizations, hobbies, and clubs. As you plan your extracurricular activities, remember that a college-entrance board is likely to be more impressed by 4 years of playing on the school soccer team than short stints on the volleyball, water polo, bowling, baseball, and fencing teams.

# Principle #190

## Use your time off from school wisely.

It might seem fun to hang out playing video games in your air-conditioned living room, but that type of summer will not get you into the college of your dreams. Use summers and other school breaks to participate in activities that will enrich your life and your college application. Participate in academic sessions held at college campuses (this is an excellent way to start a relationship with a school you hope to attend someday). Devote yourself to an artistic or athletic endeavor. Volunteer in your community. Better still, get a job that could supplement your studies and goals, such as interning at a law firm. Using your time off from school wisely can really benefit you down the academic road.

# Principle #191

## Prepare for the SATs.

※

With the exception of your GPA, your SAT scores are the most important part of your college application. Preparation for the SAT test is imperative if you want to go to college. If you can afford it, take a prep course, such as Princeton Review or Kaplan. These courses provide rigorous review of test material, offer practice exams, and help students develop test-taking strategies. Less expensive review courses are sometimes offered by high schools or academic organizations. In lieu of a course, buy a review book and commit to doing every problem in it. Daily ways to sharpen your SAT vocabulary skills include doing crossword puzzles, word games, or playing Scrabble. Visit www.collegeboard.com for more information about scores, sign-ups, and practice questions.

# Principle #192

## Take money out of the application equation.

Money is a critical part of the college process — in fact, the average cost of a year of college (including room and board) was about $12,700 in 2006. Additionally, the average cost of a private university often exceeds $30,000 a year. While money matters are serious and must be taken into consideration when accepting admission to a school, keep them out of the application process. Never refrain from applying to a school because you think you can't afford it. Get in first, then see what financial aid or grants they have to offer. In fact, many of the nation's most expensive schools are the most generous with their financial aid.

# Principle #193

## Nail the application essay.

---※---

Colleges and universities increasingly require between 1 and 3 writing samples from prospective students. Usually they ask students to answer a particular question, such as, "Describe the person you most admire," or "What would you offer our school's student body?" Admissions officers require these essays to gauge how students write and think, and also as a means to learn something unique about applicants. The application essay is an excellent opportunity to show the admissions board a side of yourself not captured in your GPA and test scores. Prepare several weeks or even months in advance to make sure your answers are innovative, unique, and comply with all directions.

# Principle #194

## Get references from people who really know you.

Letters of recommendation are not required by every school, but they are always encouraged, and always read. Get a recommendation from teachers, coaches, employers, instructors, and others who can vouch for your abilities, personality, strengths, and talents. When asking for a letter of recommendation, give plenty of advance notice. Provide a list of activities or accomplishments you have performed (while they may know you well, a list helps refresh their memory on specific dates, awards, or titles). Provide a stamped envelope addressed to the college-admissions board and you'll be on your way to a great recommendation.

# PRINCIPLE #195

## Visit as many schools as possible.

───────────── ✳ ─────────────

Brochures and Websites only tell you so much — to really experience what a college or university has to offer, you have to visit them. All colleges and universities offer daily tours during which you can explore the campus, learn about programs offered, see the facilities, and view the student body in action. The best tours are led by students who are encouraged to be frank about their experiences at the school. For a more in-depth view of a school, you can arrange with the admissions office to sit in on a class or spend the night with a current student to get an insider peek at dorm life.

# PRINCIPLE #196

## Continue the legacy.

Many colleges will give special preference to applicants whose parents attended the school. Relatives of alumni and alumnae — or legacies, as they are referred to by admissions committees — are believed to have an established affinity with the school that will help them succeed there. Furthermore, it is believed that when colleges educate several generations of the same family, they develop a warmer, closer learning environment. Almost all college applications will ask if your parents, siblings, or other close relatives are graduates of the school. If you have a family connection, don't hesitate to use it!

# Principle #197

## Apply to a wide range of schools.

───────────────── ❊ ─────────────────

College admissions committees operate with some level of predictability. By looking at average SAT scores, GPA ranges, and course curriculum requirements you can roughly predict whether you have a chance of being accepted. Research these data sets for each of the schools you like. Then, divide them into reach, safety, and match schools. Reaches are schools you are not likely, but could possibly, be accepted to. Safeties are schools you are all but guaranteed a spot at. Matches are schools for which you fall in the middle. Separating your schools into tiers will prevent you from applying only to schools out of your league or only to schools that will not challenge you enough.

# Principle #198

## Prepare for college interviews.

Many colleges offer an optional interview for prospective students. Because it is not mandatory, the interview is an often-overlooked step that could help distinguish you from other exceptional candidates applying to that college. According to a 2007 report by the National Association for College Admission Counseling, 10 percent of colleges say an applicant's interview is an important part of their application, while 34 percent factor it in to some degree. So schedule interviews with the schools you want to be accepted to. Make sure you show up for the interview on time, well dressed, and prepared to talk about skills and experiences you possess that will show the interviewer why you will be an asset to their student body.

# PRINCIPLE #199

## Apply "early decision" to your favorite college.

If you've found your dream school, consider applying "early decision," which means submitting your application before the regular deadline and finding out about your acceptance before anyone else. While only top students are advised to apply "early decision," benefits include relieving the stress of the process, saving money and time on other applications, and getting a head start on planning for college. However, understand that "early decision" means you are making a commitment to that college — you cannot apply to any other schools until you hear back from your top choice. But, if you are certain you want to attend a particular school, consider the "early decision" process.

# Principle #200

## Relax! You will get into the right school for you.

If you feel overly stressed by the college application process, you are not alone. The pressure of applying to college has become so great that a study by the Princeton Review found that 64 percent of students feel "very high" or "high" levels of stress over the college-application process. Getting into the right college is a serious matter, but not one you should be losing sleep over. To reduce your stress, just make sure you plan for college early and work hard throughout high school. With this background, you are guaranteed to get into a school that matches your abilities and interests.

# ADDITIONAL INFORMATION AND IDEAS

The following pages contain additional information and exercises that will help you become a better student. Utilizing these resources and practicing these exercises will help you develop the habits and mindset required to excel at school and get into the college or university of your choice.

These exercises will help you improve your performance in school by boosting your self-confidence, which is key to academic achievement. You will also find tools, databases, and resources that will point you in the right direction as you study, complete homework, research colleges, and send applications.

Lastly, you will find a section written especially for parents, which will give them tips and advice to further help you excel at school. Your family, and the support and love they provide, will be crucial to your continued success.

These sections provide valuable resources to help you succeed:

**• Words and Phrases that Encourage Academic Success**
Repeat the affirmations in this exercise to immediately feel better about your prospects for excelling at school.

**• Handy Websites and Resources for Students and Parents**
Visit these 15 Websites for valuable information on scholarships, college rankings, online books, research tools, and much more.

**• Foods that Support Learning**
Make sure you are eating at least 5 to 8 servings of the foods listed here to keep your body and mind in peak shape for learning and school activities.

This special section for your parents will teach your family ways to continue to support your acadamic success:

**• Ways Parents Can Help and Support Their Children**
Parents' behaviors and attitudes can monumentally impact the success children have at school. Use these tips to be sure you are creating a positive learning environment for your children.

# Words and Phrases to
# Encourage Academic Success

Practicing daily affirmations is an excellent way to boost self-esteem, a critical ingredient for academic success. Tell yourself something from this list several times a day. Don't be shy! Look in a mirror if you can while you say it. Focus on the words and how it feels to say positive, encouraging statements about yourself. When you feel the urge to say "This is stupid," force yourself to replace that thought with one of the phrases below:

- I can be a good student.
- I am competent.
- I am intelligent.
- I have done work like this before.
- I am talented.
- I am a good reader.
- I am a good writer.
- I am a capable of passing this class.

- I am a problem-solver.
- I will become more organized.
- I can change poor academic habits.
- I can succeed at whatever I try.
- I will start keeping a calendar.
- I will do all of my homework tonight.
- I can handle this assignment.
- I can do better in the future than I have done in the past.
- I will speak up in class today.
- I will manage my time better this week.
- I will maintain an assignment book.
- I will be come to class prepared today.
- I will take excellent class notes.
- I will study for and pass my tests.
- I am ready to work hard in school.
- I can develop good study skills.

# HANDY WEBSITES AND RESOURCES FOR STUDENTS AND PARENTS

**Bartleby.com** (www.bartleby.com): An incredible free resource that provides access to the *Columbia Encyclopedia*; the *Encyclopedia of World History*; the *Columbia Gazetteer of North America*; the *World Fact Book*; the *American Heritage Dictionary*; *Roget's Thesaurus*; helpful books of quotations; style guides; *Gray's Anatomy of the Human Body*; the King James Bible; and the complete works of Shakespeare, Jane Austen, J.S. Mill, and W.B. Yeats. These works are also searchable by keyword.

**CampusTours.com** (www.campustours.com): This Website offers "virtual visits" to hundreds of colleges and universities. Accompanying the virtual tours are fact sheets about each college, including student-body size, school location, and other information.

**CollegeBoard.com** (www.collegeboard.org): A database of information from the College Board on 3,300 colleges, with downloadable application forms for 1,000 schools. Students can use the site to register online for the SAT and other college-entrance exams. A helpful scholarship database and online financial aid calculator will be of particular use to parents.

**Dictionary.com** (www.dictionary.com): An easy-to-use site that compiles definitions from reputable dictionaries.

**Download.com** (www.download.com): A resource for downloading and updating software programs, many of which are free. This includes utilities for Windows, Macintosh and Linux, Internet tools, desktop dictionaries and language translators, and Pocket PC and Palm applications.

**Embark** (www.collegeedge.com): A database of information on nearly 6,000 colleges and vocational schools. Students can apply to about 300 schools online. Offers valuable scholarship information and career counseling.

**FAFSA Application** (www.fafsa.ed.gov/): Homepage for the Free Application for Federal Student Aid. A must for any family that wants to be considered for public scholarships and federally funded loans.

**FastWeb** (http://www.fastweb.com/): A scholarship service database of 180,000 private scholarships.

**FinAid!** (www.finaid.org): Comprehensive site for the National Association of Student Financial Aid Administrators. Contains information about loans, scholarships, military aid, and simplifies the complicated process of applying for financial aid.

**Flash Card Exchange** (www.flashcardexchange.com): Features flashcards on many topics and allows you to print custom cards. Also visit www.flashcardmachine.com.

**FreeTranslation.com** (www.freetranslation.com): This site converts text from one language into another, such as English to Chinese or French to English. Simply type and paste up to 10,000 characters, about 1,800 words, into the search window and then select the desired language.

**Math.com** (www.math.com): Provides help in a number of mathematics-related subjects, including basic grade-school math, calculus, algebra, geometry, trigonometry and statistics. Practice exercises are automatically graded. This free site also features a glossary, calculators, homework tips, and math games.

**Merriam-Webster** (www.m-w.com): The complete Merriam-Webster dictionary, available free online.

**Perseus Digital Library** (www.perseus.tufts.edu): Offers access to a collection of classics translated from Greek and Latin as well as literature from the English Renaissance.

**Study Tactics.com** (www.studytactics.com): Contains an exhaustive collection of top online academic resources. Sites are compiled in categories specific to areas of study, such as high school, college, vocational school, and nursing.

**Thesaurus.com** (www.thesaurus.com): A simple and easy-to-use site that compiles entries from a number of reputable thesaurauses.

**Verbix** (www.verbix.com/webverbix/index.asp): A site that helps you conjugate verbs in a variety of foreign languages.

**U.S. News & World Report School Rankings** (http://colleges.usnews.rankingsandreviews.com/usnews/edu/college/rankings/rankindex_brief.php): A site that features the current college rankings from *U.S. News & World Report* on undergraduate, graduate, public, private, liberal arts, and specialty schools.

# Foods That Support Learning

Your mental output has a lot to do with your nutritional input. The following foods have all been proven to improve brain function:

- Foods rich in omega-3 fatty acids, such as salmon, sardines, canola oil, broccoli, cauliflower, and red kidney beans keep the brain's blood vessels clear and allow nerve cells to function at a high level.

- Green leafy vegetables, almonds, and whole grains are rich in vitamin E, which protects the brain from free radicals, which are unstable damaging agents.

- Magnesium, which protects the brain from neurotoxins, is found in nuts, seeds, whole grains, and leafy green vegetables.

- Vitamin C, found in most fruits, has been shown by Johns Hopkins University researchers to cut the risk of being diagnosed with Alzheimer's disease by 64 percent. Good sources of vitamin C include oranges, lemons, limes, strawberries, cantaloupe, broccoli, red and green peppers, cauliflower, greens, grapes, tomatoes, kiwis, and berries.

- Foods rich in vitamin B12, such as mussels, clams, beef, salmon, trout, and liver, help the generation of myelin, which forms a sheath around nerve fibers in the brain.

- Foods containing vitamin B6, such as garlic, cranberries, tuna, and bell peppers, help with mood and alertness.

- Foods rich in beta-carotene — such as carrots, sweet potatoes, spinach, cantaloupe, greens, broccoli, prunes, mango, and pumpkin — improve eyesight and skin, and protect against colds, flu, and infections.

# WAYS PARENTS CAN HELP
## AND SUPPORT THEIR CHILDREN

Parents — you are uniquely positioned to impact your child's success in school. While whole libraries could be written for parents of school-aged children, here are just a few of the most important things to remember if you want to help your kids excel at school.

**Be a positive role model.** If you want your child to crack the books, you must do the same. A study collected by Malcolm Gladwell, author of the best-selling books *Blink* and *The Tipping Point*, found that homes in which parents have and read books are homes that produce children who excel in school. Teach your children that learning is a fun, rewarding, and relaxing pastime. Encourage them to read a book versus watching the movie version. Read with them. Designate times in your household that are for reading only.

Another way in which you can set an example for your school-aged child is to use high-level vocabulary in your home. Encourage your children to ask if they do not understand a word you use — then explain it, and ask them to use it in a sentence. Addtionally, be mindful of how you speak to other people. If you speak in an educated manner, chances are, so will your children. Being responsible, organized, and prompt will also help your children develop these habits and apply them at school.

**Nurture your child's self-confidence.** Self-confident students make better learners because they believe they can do it. Make sure you develop and nurture your child's self-esteem by making them feel great about whatever they are doing. Talk to them in ways that will make them feel positively supported, rather than shamed or embarrassed when they make mistakes.

Another way to boost your child's self-confidence is to be mindful of the amount of pressure you put on them. Avoid making your child's success in school the most important thing in the world. You can downplay an academic failure without ignoring it. Harping on a failure is not going to encourage a student to do better next time. In addition, it is wise to give your children places to excel outside of the classroom. Encourage them to play an instrument, join a team, or indulge in a skill-building hobby. Succeeding in any of these areas will give them the chance to feel like winners — a feeling that is bound to spill over into the classroom.

Words and phrases you can use to nurture your child's self-confidence include:

*Amazing!*
*Great job!*
*I can tell you worked hard.*
*I can tell you're really trying.*
*I knew you could do it.*
*You are improving so much.*
*Your hard work paid off!*

*I'm really proud of you.*
*Hearing this made my day!*
*You are very talented.*
*Spectacular work!*
*You amaze me.*
*You should be very proud of yourself.*

**Be involved in their schoolwork, classroom, and academic activities.** Successful students have involved parents. In order to help your children succeed academically, you must be willing to get involved in their schoolwork, classroom, and other academic activities. Get to know their teachers through one-on-one parent-teacher conferences or back-to-school nights. Sit in on their class once per semester. Learn what textbooks and readings your children are being assigned, and read along with them. This way you can foster discussion of the material in the car or over dinner. Get a copy of the course curriculum and syllabus to stay on top of what your student is learning and when his or her major assignments are due. Attend all assemblies, parent-teacher conferences, back-to-school nights, and other exhibits that will familiarize you with the activities and people in your child's classroom.

**Keep your child healthy.** In order to be in top academic shape, students need to be in top physical shape. Make sure your child eats nutritious meals and snacks. Their meals should feature at least 5 servings of fruits and vegetables, dairy, whole grains, and lean sources of protein. Encourage them to exercise and play outdoors (especially at team sports, which build character, teamwork, and camaraderie). Enforce a strict bedtime; studies show that students who get more sleep perform better on tests and in the classroom. Make sure their home learning environment is well lit and gets plenty of fresh air. Finally, help your student avoid being distracted from learning by stress by keeping family tensions to a minimum. Do discuss any upsetting news — research shows that communicating about difficult events helps children deal better with them — but avoid doing so right before a test.

**Help your children combat peer pressure.** You will probably not be your child's best friend after they are about 12 years old. Similarly, you won't always be able to be there with them when peer pressure situations arise. To help your kids fight peer pressure, provide them with venues to make good friends. Church groups, Girl and Boy Scout troops, Junior

Achievement organizations, and other clubs will surround your kids with other kids who care about being successful and who have parents that care about them.

It is dually important to get to know the children that are influencing your children. Plan activities with your kids and their friends — take them all bowling or ice skating. Get to know the parents of your childrens' friends as well. Since you can't be by your child's side at every birthday party or sleepover, becoming familiar and friendly with other parents will help you feel more comfortable when your child goes out. Seeking out parents who share your same standards and values ensures that your child will be in good hands and will have the adult support he or she needs to stand up to peer pressure.

**Show interest.** Showing interest in your child's day at school is an important part of helping him or her become a successful student. The following questions will help open up a dialogue about your child's day at school and shows that you are interested in his or her life. Make sure to listen to your child's responses fully, without interrupting. Listening lets them know that they are important and respected.

Ask these questions, or use them as starting points to think of your own:

- What do you like best about school?
- What did you like least about school today?
- What did you do for fun at school today?
- What was the hardest thing for you in school today?
- What did your teacher think of your homework/presentation/paper?
- How did you do on your test?
- How did you choose your paper topic?
- What was the most interesting thing you learned today?
- Do you know why you did not perform as well as you'd hoped on your test?

- What is your least favorite subject, and why?
- What is your favorite subject, and why?
- Who is your favorite teacher, and why?
- What books are you reading in class right now?
- Is there anything I can do to help you with your schoolwork?
- Is there a subject you'd like to consider getting tutored in?
- Do you have friends that might make good study partners?
- What homework assignments are coming up in the next week?
- Do you have any important tests or projects coming up?
- Can we make a calendar to keep track of your assignments?
- Do you want to spend some time together tonight after you finish all your homework?

**Reward your children for their hard work.** Keep a chart on the wall in your home where you track your student's progress in school and give regular rewards for improvement, a great test score, a completed project, or other milestones. While many parents try giving money for grades, studies show that rewards in the form of family time — miniature golfing, tickets to a baseball game, seeing a movie, dinner out, or even a weekend getaway — are better options. And, with many children, simple words of praise or a big hug are enough to make them smile and stay motivated.

# CONCLUSION

Congratulations! By now, you should feel good about your prospects for becoming a successful student who can achieve great things at school. *Simple Principles™ to Excel at School* has helped you develop good study habits, take effective notes, maximize time spent doing homework, and study and prepare for tests. If you follow the hints, tips, tricks, ideas, suggestions, and other principles contained in this book, you will be able to achieve your goal of becoming a better student. Now that you have gone through this book from beginning to end, you should have a solid idea of how to apply effective academic habits to your own life. The 200 principles included in this book have shown you that everyone is capable of becoming an excellent student, provided they are willing to work hard and stay motivated.

*Simple Principles™ to Excel at School* is written to help you understand that you are capable of getting great grades, enjoying the learning process, and advancing academically. Even if you find certain subjects daunting or difficult, you can get better at them by applying the principles contained in this book. From reading this book, you have learned how to become a better reader, writer, and researcher, and possess the secrets to creating a home learning environment that is conducive to studying. When you use these 200 simple principles, you will feel comfortable tackling homework that does not naturally appeal to you, and will know how to keep yourself healthy and calm to perform your best on tests.

Practice what you have learned. Keep this book handy and refer to it when you need a reminder. For instance, if you find that you are feeling stressed while studying for an upcoming test, refer back to the chapter on Getting Ready for an Exam. The tips found there will help you stay calm and maximize your preparation time. Or, if you're faced with a group of friends who seem to constantly distract you from positive study habits, or encourage bad behavior, flip to the chapter on peer pressure. Let the simple principles found there help you eliminate negative pressures and make friends that will support you and your endeavors toward success at school.

*Simple Principles™ to Excel at School* will serve as a valuable resource throughout your high school and college years, so always keep its wisdom close by. The key thing to remember is that an outstanding academic career is completely within your grasp if you just open yourself up to this new way of thinking. Remember, you can become an excellent student!

# TELL US YOUR STORY

*Simple Principles™ to Excel at School* has changed the lives of countless students, helping them study, take tests, and achieve academic success better than they ever imagined. Now we want to hear your story about how this book has improved your grades, scores, and study habits.

Tell us ...
- Why did you purchase this book?
- Which areas of your schooling did you want to improve?
- How did this book help you improve in those areas?
- How did this book change your life?
- Which principles did you like the most?
- What did you like most about this book?
- Would you recommend this book to others?

Email us your response at info@wspublishinggroup.com or write to us at:

WS Publishing Group
7290 Navajo Road, Suite 207
San Diego, CA 92119

Please include your name and an email address and/or phone number where you can be reached.

Please let us know if WS Publishing may or may not use your story and/or name in future book titles, and if you would be interested in participating in radio or TV interviews.

# Great Titles in the
# SIMPLE PRINCIPLES™ SERIES

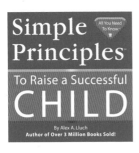

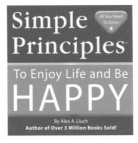

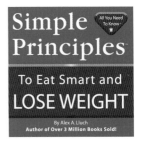

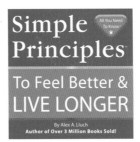

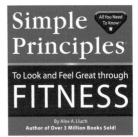

# More Great Titles in the
# SIMPLE PRINCIPLES™ SERIES

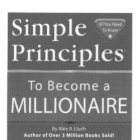

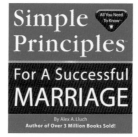

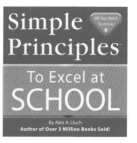

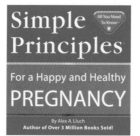

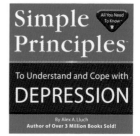

# Other Best-Selling Books
# by Alex A. Lluch

## HOME & FINANCE

- The Very Best Home Improvement Guide & Document Organizer
- The Very Best Home Buying Guide & Document Organizer
- The Very Best Home Selling Guide & Document Organizer
- The Very Best Budget & Finance Guide with Document Organizer
- The Ultimate Home Journal & Organizer
- The Ultimate Home Buying Guide & Organizer

## BABY JOURNALS & PARENTING

- The Complete Baby Journal Organizer & Keepsake
- Keepsake of Love Baby Journal
- Snuggle Bears Baby Journal Keepsake & Organizer
- Humble Bumbles Baby Journal
- Simple Principles to Raise a Successful Child

## CHILDREN'S BOOKS

- I Like to Learn: Alphabet, Numbers, Colors & Opposites
- Alexander, It's Time for Bed!
- Do I Look Good in Color?
- Zoo Clues Animal Alphabet
- Animal Alphabet: Slide & Seek the ABC's
- Counting Chameleon
- Big Bugs, Small Bugs

LOG ON TO **WSPUBLISHINGGROUP.COM** TO CHECK FOR RELEASE DATES ON THESE AND FUTURE TITLES.

# More Best-Selling Books
# by Alex A. Lluch

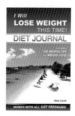

## COOKING, FITNESS & DIET

- The Very Best Cooking Guide & Recipe Organizer
- Easy Cooking Guide & Recipe Organizer
- Get Fit Now! Workout Journal
- Lose Weight Now! Diet Journal & Organizer
- I Will Lose Weight This Time! Diet Journal
- The Ultimate Pocket Diet Journal

## WEDDING PLANNING

- The Ultimate Wedding Planning Kit
- The Complete Wedding Planner & Organizer
- Easy Wedding Planner, Organizer & Keepsake
- Easy Wedding Planning Plus
- Easy Wedding Planning
- The Ultimate Wedding Workbook & Organizer
- The Ultimate Wedding Planner & Organizer

- Making Your Wedding Beautiful, Memorable & Unique
- Planning the Most Memorable Wedding on Any Budget
- My Wedding Journal, Organizer & Keepsake
- The Ultimate Wedding Planning Guide
- The Ultimate Guide to Wedding Music
- Wedding Party Responsibility Cards

LOG ON TO **WSPublishingGroup.com** TO CHECK FOR
RELEASE DATES ON THESE AND FUTURE TITLES.

# About the Author and Creator of the
# SIMPLE PRINCIPLES™ SERIES

**Alex A. Lluch** is a seasoned entrepreneur with outstanding life achievements. He grew up very poor and lost his father at age 15. But through hard work and dedication, he has become one of the most successful authors and businessmen of our time. He is now using his life experience to write the simple principles™ series to help people improve their lives.

**The following are a few of Alex's achievements:**

- Author of over 3 million books sold in a wide range of categories: health, fitness, diet, home, finance, weddings, children, and babies
- President of WS Publishing Group, a successful publishing company
- President of WeddingSolutions.com, one of the world's most popular wedding planning websites
- President of UltimateGiftRegistry.com, an extensive website that allows users to register for gifts for all occasions
- President of a highly successful toy and candy company
- Has worked extensively in China, Hong Kong, Spain, Israel and Mexico
- Designed complex communication systems for Fortune 500 companies
- Black belt in Karate and Judo, winning many national tournaments
- Owns real estate in California, Colorado, Georgia and Montana
- B.S. in Electronics Engineering and an M.S. in Computer Science

**Alex Lluch lives in San Diego, California with his wife of 16 years and their three wonderful children.**

# About the Co-Author

**Dr. Helen Eckmann** is a renowned expert in leadership, marketing, management and education. She has vast experience teaching in these fields as well as working with both small companies and Fortune 500 corporations. She is now sharing her insight and expertise in the 200 principles contained in this book.

**The following are a few of Helen's achievements:**

- Doctorate in Education and Leadership Science
- Masters in Organizational Leadership and bachelors in Management
- Consults Fortune 500 companies on leadership development
- Travels as a popular motivational speaker and mentor
- Designs and implements corporate supply chain management programs
- Serves as an Organizational Behavior Consultant to various industries
- Teaches graduate courses in business at the University of San Diego
- Has taught leadership, marketing, strategic planning, innovations and ethics to over 1,500 M.B.A. students
- Has been personnel director for several companies
- Serves on the board of directors of multiple organizations
- Founded and serves on the board of several non-profit organizations
- Provides spiritual direction to hundreds of women as a church pastor

**Dr. Helen Eckmann lives with her husband in Del Mar, California. They have raised four successful children.**